FORGIVENESS OF MAN BY MAN

In this study of *Forgiveness*, Lord Longford tackles a much neglected subject in the same spirit of enquiry in which he wrote his earlier book on *Humility*.

The doctrine of forgiveness, he insists, is central to Christianity and along with humility distinguishes Christian ethics from all other systems.

In his researches, Lord Longford found that very little had previously been written on the subject in its widest and deepest aspects. 'The principle of forgiveness', he writes, 'must be applied to both ends of the spectrum of offence – to murder at one end and to small daily annoyances at the other.'

The author has approached his subject under the following headings:

the Jewish approach to forgiveness as contrasted with that of the Christian;

forgiving and non-forgiving men;

forgiveness in literature, in politics, and specifically in Northern Ireland;

forgiveness between victim and criminal;

and the fundamental part it plays and must play in the struggle for spiritual wholeness.

The postscript on Japanese prisoners of war adds a further dimension.

In this new edition (1997) he appends an epilogue on Forgiveness and Public Policy.

LORD LONGFORD

Forgiveness of man by man

THE BUCHEBROC PRESS
Northampton · England

First published in Great Britain in 1989
by the Buchebroc Press
21 High Street, Bugbrooke
Northamptonshire NN7 3PA
This new edition with Epilogue, 1997

ISBN 1 871917 01 8

Typeset by Land & Unwin (Data Sciences) Limited
Bugbrooke, Northamptonshire
and printed in Great Britain

To my wife
ELIZABETH

Contents

Acknowledgements

My first expression of thanks must go as always to my wife, Elizabeth. After that, as many times before, to Gwen Keeble, with whom I have so long worked so closely; to Barbara Winch and Kitty Chapman for their help in preparing the manuscript, and to Matthew Oliver, with whom I have had so many fruitful discussions.

It is impossible to begin to mention the many friends and acquaintances who have helped me, directly or indirectly, over the years. I must however extend my heartfelt thanks to those mentioned in the text who allowed me to interview them. Bill Procter, for many years my valued colleague in Sidgwick & Jackson, has proved, as I knew he would, a most efficient editor.

FRANK LONGFORD
January 1989

Introduction

Some years ago I published a small book on humility. Then and since I have described it as being, along with forgiveness, the most distinctive Christian virtue. Christians may claim that additionally the concept of love is wider and deeper in the Christian faith than anywhere else. Non-Christians are liable to contest that claim. Few will deny that the claims of humility and forgiveness to be distinctively Christian are strongly based.

When writing on humility I was astonished to discover that it was (almost) impossible to find a systematic book on the subject. And that is still more or less true. For a number of years I have been under the impression that the same was true of forgiveness. For the purpose of the present book I have visited a number of bookshops, religious and other, and asked for a book on forgiveness. They could never produce one. I was aware of the existence of the *Christian Experience of Forgiveness* by Professor Mackintosh (1927). But it has long been out of print. Eventually I tracked it down in Dr Williams's library. Impressive though it is, it is concerned almost entirely with forgiveness of man by God. Forgiveness of man by man hardly figures. It is this second aspect of forgiveness which has provided the principal reason for attempting this book, although forgiveness of man by God is not neglected.

What is meant by forgiveness in ordinary usage?

When someone says to someone else, who it is believed has wronged him or her, 'I *forgive* you', he means as a minimum that he will, or at least try to, cease to feel resentment against the offender. Ideally, forgiveness opens the door to mutual understanding and love between the offender and the victim.

But forgiveness can be used in another sense equivalent to pardon. If someone *pardons* someone else as, for example, when a queen's pardon is awarded, it is implied on the human plane that punishment is not inflicted. We shall find that as between man and God matters are not so simple.

Can a person forgive another when he himself has not been injured by that other?

The issue acquires a special relevance when we turn to the forgiveness of communities by communities. If no-one could forgive anyone else who had not actually injured him, how could one community ever forgive another?

As between communities we must be very clear about our terms. There is clearly a duty on all nations ideally to seek peace and friendship with each other, whether or not they deem themselves to have been wronged by any particular country. Reconciliation is sometimes used as synonymous with forgiveness. It is also used, however, to cover the improvement in relations of any two nations who have not been getting on well. One might talk of 'reconciliation' between the United States and Soviet Russia without bringing in forgiveness. With Northern Ireland and indeed with Anglo-Irish relations generally the position is quite different. Everyone agrees that the relations between England and Ireland and between the two communities in Ireland are much bedevilled by past history, by a sense of wrong which was inflicted in the ancient or recent past.

Is there a duty to forgive when there has been no clear sign of repentance on the part of the wrongdoer?

The issue is equally acute among individuals and communities. The question, for example, confronted the Allies in their approach to Germany after World War II. In the years immediately following 1945 it was far too early for the Germans to have demonstrated their repentance and moral improvement. Should the Allies forgive them none the less? In 1947–48 I was Minister for the British Zone of Germany. I did my best to preach an unequivocal doctrine of forgiveness inspired by men like Dr Bell, Bishop of Chichester, Richard Stokes, M.P., Victor Gollancz, and Michael de la Bedoyere, editor of the *Catholic Herald*. In a sense the problem was solved by the hostility of the Soviet Union which thrust the victorious Allies and Western Germany together.

The whole question of how far forgiveness and punishment can be reconciled will be explored as I proceed. From the time (1961) when I published a small book *The Idea of Punishment* I have always accepted the necessity for punishment in a civilized society, though always believing that there is much which is inhumane in our present penal system. What meaning, however, can a prisoner, possibly serving a long sentence, attach to any official statement that he has been forgiven?

Ireland. Germany. Prisoners.

Here are three areas where my own life has made me acutely aware of the urgent problems of forgiveness. Others will have suffered in a way that I have been spared at the hands of wrongdoers. But whether the issue comes to us in public or private guise I am sure that few of us go through life without encountering it in one form or another.

I said earlier that this book will be mainly concerned with forgiveness of man by man. But it is, of course, impossible (in the case of Christianity at least) to separate that aspect from forgiveness of man by God. 'Forgiveness', wrote Professor Mackintosh in *The Christian Experience of Forgiveness*, 'is central in Christianity. It is a truth and ingredient without which the faith created by Jesus Christ would lose its identity. With the Lord there is mercy and with Him is plenteous redemption. This is the note of authentic Christianity.' What is written above can be accepted by Christians of all denominations.

The Jews have a double claim on our most earnest attention. On the one hand Jesus Christ, the founder of the

Christian religion, was a Jew steeped in the Old Testament. On the other hand they have experienced unparalleled suffering at the hands of their fellow men in this century, to go no further back. We shall begin our study with them in the first chapter.

CHAPTER ONE

The Jewish approach to forgiveness

The illustrious Jewish theologian Rabbi Louis Jacobs kindly allowed me to call on him in my attempt to understand the Jewish approach to forgiveness. We were both aware, he vastly more than I, that forgiveness of man by God is a doctrine running through the Old Testament. I ventured to submit, however, that forgiveness of man by man was a novel doctrine when presented by Jesus Christ. Rabbi Jacobs understood my reasons for saying that. He insisted, however, that the same essential message is to be found in the early Talmud (AD 200). He insisted moreover that there is no reason whatever to suppose that the authors of the Talmud derived their doctrine from Christian teaching. He was satisfied that they had arrived at it quite independently.

I would not of course dream of arguing with Rabbi Jacobs, or indeed any rabbi about the Talmud. But as far as I can make out, the doctrine of forgiveness of man by man looms very small in those many volumes. When it is stated it would hardly satisfy Christians. 'Transgressions', we read in the Talmud, 'between man and The Place (a word used for God) the Day of Atonement expiates. Transgressions between man and his neighbour the Day of Atonement does not expiate until his companion be reconciled.' There does seem to be a real distinction here between the Jewish and Christian approaches.

The contrast between Christian and Jewish attitudes in regard to forgiveness was thrashed out in *The Times* with clarity and charity in 1985 and 1986. The controversy was set off by the visit of President Reagan to the Nazi S.S. graves in May 1985. Dr Friedlander, editor of *European Judaism*, then and later played a leading part in the public discussion. As a child of eleven in 1939 he was arrested in Berlin, his home city. He escaped with his family to Cuba and later to the United States. He is now Dean of Leo Baeck College and minister of the Westminster Synagogue.

His striking contribution in *The Times* of 4 May 1985 begins with the affirmation: 'the holocaust must not be forgotten'. He admits that, 'let us forgive and forget is a central thought within our society'. But he says that, 'it is addressed mainly to the Jews' and he refuses to agree for a moment that the Jews can now *forgive* their persecutors. 'Can we forgive', he asks. 'Who are we to usurp God's rule?' He then tells a striking anecdote, which many Christians will find disturbing.

> Some years ago speaking at a Church Conference at Nuremberg he talked about the anguish of Auschwitz. An elderly man approached him: 'Rabbi', he said, 'I was a guard at a concentration camp. Can you forgive me?' I looked at him. 'No', I said, 'I cannot forgive. It is not the function of rabbis to give absolution, to be pardoners. In Judaism there is a ten-day period of Penitence, between the New Year and the Day of Atonement, when we try to go to any person whom we have wronged, and ask for forgiveness. But you cannot go to the six million. They are dead, and I cannot speak for them. Nor can I speak for God. But you are here at a church conference. God's forgiving grace may touch you; but I am not a mediator, pardoner, or spokesman for God.'

I will return later to a fuller exposition of Rabbi Friedlander's attitude as set out in an article in *Christian Jewish Relations* in 1986. However, I must mention first that a vigorous correspondence followed in *The Times* about which Rabbi Friedlander commented subsequently: 'The texts often show a total failure of communication. Reading the correspondence one cannot possibly ignore the sharp difference between the Christian and Jewish attitudes.' The Christian standpoint was powerfully expressed by Canon Phillips, Chaplain of St John's College, Oxford, under the heading 'Why the Jews Should Forgive'. The concluding passage which aroused a good deal of resentment among Jewish contributors ran as follows: 'To remember and not to forgive can only invite further bloodshed, as the history of Ulster confirms. A theology unwilling to come to terms with the oppressors, however heinous their crimes, imprisons itself in its own past, jeopardizing the very future it would ensure. Without forgiveness there can be no healing within the community, no wholeness, holiness. For failure to forgive is not a neutral act: it adds to the sum total of evil in the world and dehumanizes the victims in a way the oppressors could never on their own achieve. In remembering the Holocaust, Jews hope to prevent its recurrence, by declining to forgive, I fear that they unwittingly invite it.'

To return to Dr Friedlander and his article, 'Judaism and the Concept of Forgiving'. He writes, 'In the Jewish tradition we begin by asking: what does God require of the sinner? How can the sinner achieve forgiveness? Let him bring a sin offering, and his guilt will be atoned! Sin is an uncleanness which adheres to the malefactor; and the vocabulary of forgiveness is replete with such verbs as *tiher* (purify), *machah* (wipe), *kibbes* (wash), *kipper* (purge) and God removes that sin from the guilty party.'

Tremendous emphasis is laid from the beginning on the need for the sinner to put himself right with God. The Rabbi stresses the fact that Judaism, unlike Christianity, is opposed to original sin. But I cannot feel that this difference in itself is responsible for the main divergence in regard to forgiveness. Here is one of the cardinal passages in Dr Friedlander's article:

> 'The winning of forgiveness depends upon the action of the sinner. The wrong done must be acknowledged and confessed. It must have become abhorrent to the sinner. The sinner must change before receiving forgiveness and public acts of fasting and self-abasement must be followed by actions demonstrating a change of heart and new way of life. The sinner and the one who has suffered from the sin cannot come back to each other until the sinner has turned in repentance in total sincerity.'

Later in the same essay Rabbi Friedlander insists that the Jewish world is not consumed with hate and feelings of revenge. He cannot, however, resist indicating the scale of the atrocities undergone . . . He concludes: 'Gently but firmly we have to point out that the actions needed to secure pardon for these crimes must initially come from the perpetrators – and they must be placed before the altar of God. Then and only then and as individuals rather than one collective might we begin to say words of comfort to our neighbours. But not yet . . . not yet.'

On this analysis how can the Jews ever forgive the present Germans whatever acts of redemption the latter perform?

The main perpetrators of the crimes are either dead or so old that they are in no position to make effective atonement. When the concentration camp guard approached Rabbi Friedlander he must be thought to have repented. His presence at a church conference suggested that his acts were corresponding to his good intentions. But still the Rabbi told him, and feels sure that he was right to tell him, that only God could forgive him. If this is to be the last word on the subject it would, on the fact of it, make nonsense of all community attempts to forgive one another.

One is left asking whether the Jewish attitude to those responsible for the Holocaust should be regarded as the long-term attitude of Judaism to forgiveness? If Rabbi Jacobs is right, the Jewish attitude and the Christian attitude to forgiveness are similar or even identical. If Rabbi Friedlander is right, there is, at the present moment at least, a great gulf fixed between Jewish and Christian attitudes. But perhaps as the unspeakable horrors of the Holocaust become less overwhelming in memory, the two theologies may draw closer together.

Nothing written above should fail to emphasize the Christian debt to the Jews for the doctrine of *compassion* which is so prominent in the Old Testament, and in later Jewish thought. I showed this chapter to Rabbi Friedlander who went to much trouble to comment on it. All too briefly I must report some of the propositions he advanced.

Collective forgiveness is a fundamental idea in Jewish thought. Many scholars point out that the Old Testament 'in contrast to the New' stresses collective thinking, collective responsibility, and thus collective forgiveness. 'The New Testament deals more with the individual.' Rabbi Friedlander goes on to point out that 'God holds Israel responsible for its sins since the people entered into the covenant at Sinai and freely took obligations upon itself. If they sin, they are punished. If they repent, they are forgiven. God is abundant in grace and all-forgiving, but the stress is placed upon repentance preceding this.'

In Dr Friedlander's view, which I am taking as representative of Judaism, in The Bible *only God* HAS JUDGED A PEOPLE GUILTY, and *only God* HAS FORGIVEN A PEOPLE. Can humans usurp that role?

This leads him on to repeat his refusal to agree that Israel could or should forgive Germany for its collective guilt. What collective guilt?, he asks. 'We are not God to make our judgement.' He would now appear to be saying that the Jews can neither condemn the Germans as a whole nor forgive them. Presumably this would apply to any relationship of this kind between any two countries.

Dr Friedlander asks, 'Can a person forgive those who have wronged others?' (This question is, incidentally, brought up against me when I befriend well-known prisoners.) His reply is an unhesitating 'No.' He admits that the story of Jonah, who was asked to forgive the people of Nineveh, brings us closer together. 'Not, however, all the way,' because in that case Nineveh had already been forgiven by God.

The deepest difference between Dr Friedlander and myself, a representative Jew and a far from representative Christian, is his insistence that 'repentance precedes forgiving'. He puts in the thought-provoking comment '*We* say repentance precedes forgiving; you start from the other side. One of the many flaws I find in the Christian position here is that the unrepentant sinner neither wants nor needs forgiveness.' 'How can you forgive me,' he says. 'I've done nothing wrong.'

Christians will surely say that the act of love involved in forgiving the sinner, repentant or unrepentant, is itself an instrument for good, of benefit to oneself, to the sinner, and who knows to how many others.

CHAPTER TWO

The Christian approach to forgiveness

Whatever may be the case with other creeds, the doctrine of 'Forgiveness' is essential to Christianity. Christianity tells us that God took human form in Jesus Christ, that he showed a special concern for sinners, and died on the cross to redeem sinful mankind.

Take first, forgiveness of man by man. The Gospels are permeated through and through with our duty to forgive one another. When Peter asked Christ, 'How often shall my brother sin against me, and I forgive him? As many as seven times?' Jesus replied, 'I do not say to you seven times, but seventy times seven' (Matt. 18: 21–2). In other words, indefinitely. He said to the accusers of the woman taken in adultery, 'Let him who is without sin among you be the first to throw a stone' (John 8:11). And to the woman herself, 'Neither do I condemn you' (John 8:11). That last phrase has been used quite often in recent times as a reason for not condemning anything at all; for being, to use the modern jargon, non-judgemental.

We should, however, remember that Christ said to the same woman, 'Go and do not sin again' (John 8:11). In other words he did not fail to condemn the sin because he loved the sinner. As he hung in agony from the cross he prayed for his tormentors, 'Father, forgive them for they know not what they do' (Luke 23:34). And to the penitent thief he gave this assurance, 'Today you will be with me in Paradise' (Luke 23:43).

Every time a Christian says the Lord's Prayer, he uses the words 'Forgive us our trespasses, as we forgive those who trespass against us.' Instructions such as those to love our enemies and turn the other cheek are part of the same message. In short, Christianity and forgiveness are so wrapped up together that they cannot be separated.

I now turn to forgiveness of man by God and begin with Professor Mackintosh's book *The Christian Experience of Forgiveness*, mentioned earlier, 'Forgiveness', he sums up in his final chapter, ' is essential in Christianity; it is an ingredient, without which the faith created by Jesus Christ would lose its identity. . . . Had not the Gospel held this blessing at its heart, we should not have been able to recount the triumph of Christianity over other less sufficient worships. . . . To forgive, on God's part, is in pure love to draw the sinner, despite his sin, into communion with Himself . . . .' And somewhat earlier he is almost more emphatic, 'The heart must be thrown open by the welcome certainty of forgiveness before the long process of what has usually been called sanctification can begin.'

As one reads this book and returns to it for re-reading, one asks oneself continually; What is he asserting beyond the fact that God is all-loving? The answer would appear to be that he is explaining how the love of God operates in coping with the sinfulness of man. He never lets us forget this human sinfulness. God, if we may put it that way without irreverence, is now confronted with the problem, so well known in human affairs, of hating the sin and loving the sinner. The answer provided by Mackintosh is challenging. 'The point is that the divine character is such that wherever it encounters moral evil, in saint or sinner, it cannot but react against it with repelling and retributive force. Love, that is worthy to be called love, confronts the evil thing with an inevitable and intrinsic purity. If God did not chastise sin in the very act of forgiveness, and in the persons of the forgiven as a sequel to forgiving them, He would not be more loving than He is; He would cease to be God.'

Pardon, according to Mackintosh, does not automatically involve the abolition of punishment. The truth, rather, is that over a certain area of experience pardon and retribution invariably go together because the holy love that constitutes the Father's very being, makes anything else impossible. Forgiveness by God is impossible unless man has played his part in expressing his penitence in words and deeds. But it would also be impossible if Jesus Christ had not laid down his life for us by his death on the Cross, so overcoming human evil by a supreme act of love and sacrifice.

Professor Mackintosh devotes a very closely argued chapter to the Atonement. He shows himself fully aware of the intellectual arguments hostile to the notion. One of his pages is headed 'Is Atonement Immoral?' He asks, 'How can we worthily conceive the transference of ethical responsibilities from one person to another?' His answer, he acknowledges, is likely to be more convincing to Christians than to non-Christians. We could not arrive at a doctrine of the atonement by a priori philosophical reason. We can only reach it through an understanding of Jesus Christ as he reveals himself in the Gospels.

In Mackintosh's exposition the death of Christ is not just an overwhelmingly inspiring example. In itself as a supreme act of love and sacrifice it goes far to overcome the sinfulness of human beings. It makes it possible for us to be reconciled to God if we play our own part in humility and penitence. He nevertheless accepts the difficulty of replying to the objection above. How can we worthily conceive the transference of ethical responsibilities from one person to another. He answers it in effect by saying that through our own incorporation in Christ we share in the infinite value of this sacrifice.

It is probable that Protestants and Catholics can unite in supporting teaching of this kind but Roman Catholics, and many others who would describe themselves as Catholics, treasure a more elaborate doctrine. The Reformers, it has been said by one authority, upholding the doctrine of justification by faith, held that repentance consisted in a change of the whole moral attitude of the mind and soul (Matt. 8:15, Luke 22:32) and that the Divine forgiveness followed true repentance and confession to God without any reparation of 'works'. For Roman Catholics the sacrament of penance consists of three parts; *contritio, confessio, satisfactio. Contritio* is in fact repentance as Protestant theologians understand it, that is, sorrow for sin arising from love of God; but 'reconciliation' can not follow such contrition without the other parts of the sacrament, which form part of it. The word 'penance', applied to the whole sacrament, is also used of the works of satisfaction imposed by the priest on the penitent, that is, the temporal punishment (*poena*).

We do not need to dwell on the question of how far the function of purgatory is punitive and how far purgative. My own emphasis, for what it is worth, falls increasingly on the latter. Nor can we here attempt to probe the nature of the sinfulness which we ask God to forgive.

Professor Mahoney in an important section of his book *The Making of Moral Theology* has argued that the development of the early Church with 'auricular confession' has led to a preoccupation with sin and legality. 'It was the Church's growing tradition of moral theology', he writes, 'which was itself heavily responsible for increasing men's weakness and moral apprehension, with the strong sense of sin and guilt which it so thoroughly strove to inculcate or reinforce, and the humiliations and punishments with which it drove its message home.'

Professor Mahoney reminds us that Christianity is above all a religion of love and that our failures are failures in love.

Many of us, especially as we grow older, are more conscious of inadequacy than of breaking explicit rules. That does not however diminish our awareness of our need to be forgiven by God.

When we turn to forgiveness of *man by man* we look to C. S. Lewis to provide a lucid and quasi official summary. He does not let us down. 'We believe', he wrote, 'that God forgives us our sins; but also that he will not do so unless we forgive other people their sins against us. There is no doubt about the second part of this statement. It is in the Lord's Prayer; it was emphatically stated by our Lord. If you don't forgive you will not be forgiven.' The trouble, he goes on to say, is that what we call asking God's forgiveness very often really consists in asking God to accept our excuses. And 'there is all the difference in the world between forgiving and excusing'. When it comes to forgiving other people it is still true that forgiving does not mean excusing. We must hate the sin but love the sinner. C. S. Lewis insists, I am sure correctly, that 'To be a Christian means to forgive the inexcusable because God has forgiven the inexcusable in us.' So far we go along with Lewis, but now he goes too far, for me at any rate. 'Does loving your enemy mean not punishing him? No, for loving myself does not mean that I ought not to subject myself to punishment – even to death. If one had committed a murder, the right Christian thing to do would be to give oneself up to the police and be hanged. It is, therefore, in my opinion, perfectly right for a Christian judge to sentence a man to death or a Christian soldier to kill an enemy.'

One cannot tell whether Lewis would have written in the same way at the present time when capital punishment has been abolished for twenty-five years. A further passage in this particular essay shows a kind of limitation.

Lewis says that when we are told to love our enemy that means to wish him good not to feel fond of him. I myself would hold that love is less abstract, more emotional than that.

He has a good deal more to say about forgiveness but always incidentally to his main themes. At no point does he contribute to a clarification of the three difficult questions.

Can one forgive those who have not injured one directly or indirectly?
Must we forgive those who have not repented?
How do we reconcile forgiveness with punishment, which may be imprisonment for years?

No layman has done as much as Lewis in this century to expound Christian doctrine with ingenuity, piety, and literary skill. But he is at his weakest on forgiveness. And the reason is not far to seek. Christian doctrine on forgiveness of *man by man* as distinct from forgiveness of *man by God* remains undeveloped. It was impossible for Lewis to expound the official doctrine because there wasn't any to expound.

I am assured by my theological friends that however deeply I plunge into Augustine, Aquinas, and Luther, for instance, I shall not find answers to my questions. So in later chapters I shall be turning mainly to individual Christians who have practised forgiveness or failed to practise it.

INTERLUDE

The Koran

For Muslims the Koran is the infallible Word of God revealed to the prophet Mohammed about the end of the sixth century AD. I have re-read it with a view to find out what relevance if any it has to a book on forgiveness. The answer seems plain enough. To a discussion of man's forgiveness by God, plenty of relevance. To man's forgiveness by man, very little. Every chapter begins 'In the Name of Allah, the Compassionate the Merciful' which raises our hopes. Chapter 40 is entitled 'The Forgiving One'. 'This book we are told by Allah, the Mighty One, the All-Knowing, who forgives sin and accepts repentance; the Bountiful One, whose punishment is stern.' Much of the chapter is devoted to a horrifying account of the fate of unbelievers. 'Do you not see how those who dispute the revelations of Allah turn away from the right path? Those who have denied the Scriptures and the message with which We have sent Our apostles shall know the truth hereafter: when with chains and shackles round their necks they shall be dragged through boiling water and burnt in the fire of Hell.' The duty of seeking forgiveness from God is stressed repeatedly. 'Seek forgiveness of your Lord and turn to him in repentance. He will make a goodly provision for you till an appointed day and will bestow His grace upon the righteous. But if you give no heed, then beware of the torment of a fateful day. To Allah you shall all return. He has power over all things.'

But the references to the forgiveness of *man by man* are indeed hard to come by. There are not in fact a great many passages which contain ethical as distinct from theological instruction. I will quote two to indicate the flavour. 'Blessed are the believers, who are humble in their prayers, who avoid profane talk, and give alms to the destitute; who restrain their carnal desires (except with wives and slave-girls, for these are lawful to them) and do not transgress through lusting after other women; who are true to their trusts and promises and never neglect their prayers. These are the heirs of Paradise; they shall abide in it for ever.' Later on we read, 'Righteousness does not consist in whether you face towards the east or the west. The righteous man is he who believes in Allah and the Last Day, in the angels and the Scriptures and the prophets; who for the love of Allah gives his wealth to his kinsfolk, to the orphans, to the needy, to the wayfarers and to the beggars, and for the redemption of captives; who attends to his prayers and pays the alms-tax; who is true to his promises and steadfast in trial and adversity and in times of war. Such are the true believers; such are the God-fearing.' It is difficult to extract anything of significance for my purpose from passages such as these. One can come across an occasional phrase which is more suggestive. This one for example: 'To endure with fortitude and to forgive is a duty incumbent on all.' But the previous short paragraph delivers a different message: 'Those who avenge themselves when wronged incur no guilt.'

Whatever the other merits of the Koran, it seems to have nothing to contribute to the study of forgiveness of *man by man*

And the same is true of the other great religions (apart from Judaism already considered).

CHAPTER THREE

Forgiving and non-forgiving men

FORGIVING MEN

GANDHI

It is impossible in a book on forgiveness not to deal with Mahatma Gandhi. We think of him instinctively as a great forgiving man. We come across this passage in his *Collected Life and Thoughts:*

> 'Have I that non-violence of the brave in me? My death alone will show that. If someone killed me and I died with prayer for the assassin on my lips, and God's remembrance and consciousness of His living presence in the sanctuary of my heart, then alone would I be said to have had the non-violence of the brave.'

He repeated the thought on a number of occasions. When he was shot on the night of 29 January, 1948, one does not doubt that if it had been physically possible he would have forgiven his assassin in the same way as Jesus Christ. It is tempting to think of him as 'forgiving Britain' for wrongs done to India. Many Indians would have seen his attitude in that light though not Gandhi himself.

It is not easy, however, to link Gandhi's non-violence with forgiveness as understood by Christians. Certainly his belief in God permeated his life. 'I have made', he said, 'the world's faith in God my own and as my faith is ineffaceable I regard that faith as amounting to experience. And is this power benevolent or malevolent? I see it as purely benevolent. For I can see that in the midst of death life persists, in the midst of untruth truth persists, in the midst of darkness light persists. Hence I gather that God is Life, Truth, Light. He is Love. He is the Supreme God.'

Yet though he had a deep reverence for Jesus Christ as a holy man among other holy men he did not think of God as personal nor Jesus Christ as Divine. The Christian connection between our forgiveness by God and our duty to forgive our fellow men was not significant for him.

Taking, however, the Sermon on the Mount as a whole we can feel that Gandhi expressed the same spirit. The passages of Matthew 25 about loving our enemies and turning the other cheek are reflected whether consciously or not in Gandhi's teaching 2,000 years later.

How does this close similarity come about? Gandhi certainly set out to love all men equally. 'I believe in the absolute oneness of God and, therefore, of humanity,' he wrote. 'What though we have many bodies? We have but one soul. The rays of the sun are many through refraction. But they have the same source. I cannot, therefore, detach myself from the wickedest soul nor may I be denied identity with the most virtuous.'

Even the greatest saints did not live up to that aspiration at all times but that at least was the standard by which Gandhi came to judge himself.

I have not yet touched on what he himself regarded as his greatest spiritual contribution – *ahimsa* or non-violence. He becomes so lyrical about *ahimsa* that one can only quote his words without claiming that one understands his full meaning.

'Ahimsa and Truth are so intertwined that it is practical-

> ly impossible to disentangle and separate them. They are like the two sides of a coin, or rather a smooth unstamped metallic disc. Who can say, which is the obverse, and which the reverse? Nevertheless, ahimsa is the means; Truth is the end. Means to be means must always be within our reach, and so ahimsa is our supreme duty. If we take care of the means, we are bound to reach the end sooner or later. When once we have grasped this point final victory is beyond question. Whatever difficulties we encounter, whatever apparent reverses we sustain, we may not give up the quest for Truth which alone is, being God Himself.'

Any sincere practitioner of ahimsa would be inevitably forgiving in the sense he would not bear resentment against anyone, whether or not he had been wronged by him. Some Christian exponents of forgiveness today, such as Canon Oestreicher, are pacifists, a majority perhaps are not. There is no necessary connection in logic between forgiveness and pacifism or non-violence. Christians generally, however, will draw much inspiration from Gandhi's approach to the task of loving everyone, enemies included.

Gandhi might have been dismissed as a delightful theorist if he had functioned only as a guru remote from the world. His influence on the politics of the world during this century, not only of India has been unmistakeable and enduring. He never ruled India, however, nor managed a large concern other than a political party engaged in protest. He does not, therefore, leave us a legacy of how to apply forgiveness, or for that matter non-violence, to questions of administration or justice.

VICTOR GOLLANCZ

Victor Gollancz must feature in any book dealing with forgiveness in the twentieth century. He never wrote a systematic book on that or indeed on any subject, although he wrote much and powerfully. But at certain moments he expressed in word and deed the ideal of forgiveness more effectively and more dramatically than any man of my time.

Twenty years ago I wrote that Victor Gollancz (1893–1967) had influenced me more that anyone outside my family, my teachers, and my Church. I would certainly say the same today. Victor did not have charisma in the ordinary sense. He charmed many but he also repelled many, including it would seem Lord Attlee, a good relationship with whom would have been much to his advantage. He had, however, an extraordinary force of personality allied to a unique capacity for feeling strongly about public causes and for expressing those feelings with immediate eloquence.

Sometime in 1962 I happened to see a photograph in *The Times* of Sir Oswald Mosley, by that time elderly, being trodden underfoot by a London crowd at one of his meetings. Immediately I thought of Victor and hastened round to see him. Within a few minutes, he had drafted a trenchant letter which appeared over our joint signatures in *The Times* next day. I was one of many who felt confident that if he espoused a cause there would be no doubt about the impact.

Victor was concerned with many campaigns, of which I will mention only a few. In the thirties he was the driving force behind the Left Book Club and the immensely successful propaganda which undoubtedly played a significant part in the Labour triumph of 1945. But forgiveness did not figure in that prolonged attack on Fascism abroad and Chamberlain at home. Victor, though he never became a Communist, worked closely with them throughout that period (I was doing the same myself on a smaller scale in Oxford). By the beginning of 1939, as he told me on the way back from France, he was becoming disillusioned with Soviet Russia. The Nazi-Soviet Pact at the end of August in that year traumatically completed the process. Even so, he published in *Guilty Men* a merciless assault on the men of Munich. No sign yet of a forgiving nature.

His finest hours were to begin with the end of the war. He had already expressed strong criticism of any idea of imposing a Carthaginian peace on the Germans. Early in September 1945 he took the initiative leading to the establishment of the 'Save Europe Now' movement. It was intended to help all who were close to starvation in Europe, but more particularly the Germans. A letter over his and other distinguished signatures appeared in the *Daily Herald*, the *Manchester Guardian* and the *News Chronicle*. It was full of gruesome details, this one for example: 'A hoard of Germans is struggling daily into Berlin and being turned away because there is no food for them. The majority are old men, women and children.' The letter ended: 'We ask therefore all who read this letter, and who share our concern, immediately to send a postcard (not a letter) to "Save Europe Now", 144, Southampton Row, London W.C.1, giving their name and address and saying that they will gladly have their rations cut, if thereby alone men, women and children of whatever nationality may be saved from intolerable suffering.' The postcards arrived, 30,000 within the month, 60,000 by early 1946 and 100,000 by the spring.

Victor kept up the pressure unceasingly. A year later he spent six weeks in the British Zone of Germany and on his return produced a damaging indictment of the whole British administration. At that time I was an Under-Secretary at the War Office and called on to defend the Government's performance. Though an accepted friend of Victor, I was duly lambasted by him.

In the spring of the following year I became Minister for the British Zone and tried desperately to advocate Christian principles, even where I had not got the power to put them into practice. Victor was at once a powerful inspiration and a remorseless goad. One way and another, he achieved far more than any other individual for stricken Germany. There were others, Dick Stokes, MP, the Bishop of Chichester, and the Editor of the *Catholic Herald* who said the same things. But no-one could match Victor for the way in which he seized the high moral ground in an argument.

He made those opposed to him, not infrequently, feel guilty; which produced results but made him enemies in high quarters.

His reputation in Germany rose to great heights and was maintained for many years. In the spring of 1953, the German government conferred on him the highest honour in its gift, the Order of Merit. It was the first time it had been awarded to a non-German. He was informed by an interviewer that every German visitor to London was inclined to ask, 'There are two things I want to see in London, Buckingham Palace and Mr. Victor Gollancz.' During the next two years, three German cities named streets after him. The fact that he was a Jew added to the excitement, though it did him no good with the Jewish community.

I would certainly describe him as the apostle of forgiveness in the sense that he, more than anyone, assisted the Bitish people to forgive their former enemies. But I seldom heard him speak of forgiveness as representing his own attitude. He was at all times the international humanitarian who believed all men were brothers.

His dedicated work for Germany and his growing friendship with Canon John Collins bore fruit in what, looking back, was a startling adventure for someone always referred to as a leading Jew. In December 1946, Christian Action was founded and came into being with a very successful meeting in the Oxford Town Hall. A second great public meeting was held in November 1947 in the Sheldonian Theatre. Victor was the star speaker. Without dissent, the following resolution was passed at the end.

> 'We Christians present at this meeting, having heard the challenge made by Victor Gollancz, resolve and call upon all Christians to support us in our resolution to do

> all in our power to make the principle of reconciliation operative to the maximum degree possible in our national policy towards Germany and all other needy countries.'

Was any greater tribute ever paid by a Christian audience to a Jew?

But the Church of England newspaper was critical. 'Some may well be puzzled,' they asked, 'whether a Jew or a Christian was speaking.' Victor Gollancz took umbrage at a later comment in the paper: 'It surely seems strange that a preacher who is commonly regarded as a Jew, should preach a view about man that he presumably does not accept.' He insisted in his reply that, 'Thou shalt love thy neighbour as thyself' was a Jewish doctrine long before it was Christian. He went on, however, 'Christian ethics, properly understood, developed the Jewish ethics they took over into something spiritually far deeper and, in the best sense far more uncompromising'. The truth is that Victor Gollancz, though brought up a strict Jew, had reacted long since against Jewish theology. But he could not by any stretch of the imagination be called a believing Christian, though deeply versed in the theology of that religion. As his brilliant biographer Ruth Dudley Edwards points out, there was never any possibility that he would be baptized. He could not be said to believe in the divinity of Christ.

Two other campaigns of Victor Gollancz must be mentioned here before I come to his persistent attempts to enlighten Jewry. He played a prominent part in a campaign, ultimately successful, that led to the abolition of capital punishment; but others, Gerald Gardiner (now Lord Gardiner) had much more long-term influence. The same kind of thing could be said of his association with the Campaign for Nuclear Disarmament, where he felt that he had been unfairly excluded from the initial proceedings. His relations with his fellow Jews, however, would make a book in themselves. When the Jews were establishing their independence and at the same time routing the Arabs, Victor went to extreme limits in the cause of Arab relief. Already, as mentioned above, his passionate concern for the stricken Germans was damaging him in Jewish eyes. When the Anglo-German Association (of which I was for some time Chairman) was founded, Victor's name appeared among those supporting it.

He had been invited to a meeting in Brighton of the Friends of the Hebrew University of Jerusalem, but was informed that the meeting 'would not meet with financial success owing to the recent news that you are connected with the newly-formed Anglo-German Association'. His visit therefore was cancelled.

I have said that Victor Gollancz did not attempt to provide a systematic theory of forgiveness. He dealt happily and fluently with abstractions in the moral area but he never sought to codify his thought in a series of propositions. If, however, we wish to understand how he approached forgiveness in practice, we must linger over his pamphlet 'The Case of Adolph Eichmann'. In most of his other campaigns even though he was usually pursuing 'an unpopular course' he had behind him a volume of strong, even passionate, minority feelings. When he fought for justice to Eichmann he fought alone. His pamphlet was eventually acclaimed by the Christian press. It caused vast outrage to the Jews collectively speaking.

At the time it appeared, May 1961, Eichmann was about to be tried. It was almost certain that he would be executed. Victor Gollancz began by contradicting the argument brought forward by the Israeli Prime Minister Ben-Gurion that the trial of Eichmann would in some way have a beneficial effect on young Jews in particular. Victor asseverated, in my eyes convincingly, that the effect would be precisely the opposite.

The Jews of all ages already knew only too well the appalling sufferings of their poeple at the hands of the Nazis. To keep alive the memory was to stir up nothing but hatred. He dwelt at length on the unfairness of any trial of Eichmann by legal standards and then posed the question 'Is Eichmann guilty?' He involved himself in a lengthy discussion of how far any of us have free will. He concluded that we have it in a limited measure but he declined to discuss the guilt of Eichmann without dwelling at length on the guilt of the Allies who directly or indirectly shared so much of the responsibility for the emergence of Hitler and in due course of Eichmann. He summed up idiosyncratically: 'Eichmann sinned beyond measure: but whether he was also guilty, in the only sense I can give to the word, neither I nor Mr. Ben-Gurion, nor the Court of his judges now sitting in Israel, can ever know.'

So far Victor Gollancz's approach might seem to be somewhat semantic, though it would lead us in the spirit of the Gospel to hesitate before throwing the first stone. In the last quarter of the pamphlet he faces the practical issue '. . . now, as I consider what sentence should follow his inevitable conviction, I shall assume him fully accountable for everything he did – by way of obeying his master as well as by gratuitous bestialities: I shall assume him, in the strict sense, in my sense, guilty.'

He quotes one of his favourite poets, William Blake.

'What shall I do? What could I do if I could find these
Criminals?
I could not dare to take vengeance, for all things are so
constructed
And builded by the Divine hand that the sinner shall
always escape,
And he who takes vengeance alone is the criminal of
Providence.'

Then he puts to himself the crucial question; 'Should Eichmann be killed?' and finds in Blake as in Jesus the uncompromising answer: six million times no. He is brought at once to consider whether the punishment of death is ever justified and considers that two main arguments have been induced in favour of it. One the deterrent argument, and two the argument for what he calls retributive or compensatory justice. In Eichmann's case he dismisses the argument for deterrence: 'The deterrent value of the death penalty has never as far as I am aware been adduced as among the reasons for killing Eichmann.'

Then he goes on, 'the death penalty is defended on a second and far more serious ground. It satisfies in certain cases, people more or less obscurely feel – and there have been theologians to agree with them – a retributive or compensatory justice that is somehow demanded by God (or the whole scheme of things) and for which men are required to act as the agents.' He has no doubt at all what we all ought to think about this second argument: 'the whole idea of compensatory or retributive justice – the notion that the very nature of things demands a blow for a blow – is not only false, it is based on the ultimate lie.'

Therefore, no intelligent or humane person ought to entertain a retributive theory of punishment. No such person ought to believe or say that Eichmann because of his unparalleled crimes deserved to be executed. Thus writes Victor. Here I must bring in my own conclusions which were initially expressed in that same year, 1961, in a small book called *The Idea of Punishment*. I found room, and would still find room for the idea that the severity of a punishment should be linked to the gravity of the offence. But I found equal room for other ideas, still more demanding, among them deterrence and rehabilitation. According to this way of thinking any theory of retribution which ruled out rehabilitation, the death penalty for example, must itself be ruled out from the beginning.

Victor Gollancz did not argue in quite that way. His purpose was idealistic but immensely practical. I repeat that we must not discuss his view of forgiveness as though he were writing an academic treatise. It is best to quote a passage from his own conclusions.

'I must try to sum up. I find a law in my spirit that

banishes all arguments to nothingness, and it is this. In no possible circumstances may you treat a fellow creature despitefully, however unspeakable his own despitefulness towards others: in no possible circumstances may you measure out tit for tat and indulge in retributive vengeance. If a man has killed one of his fellows, you may not kill him in return: if a man has killed six million of his fellows, you may not kill him in return. That is why I say to Ben-Gurion, with the deepest sympathy and respect, "Do not kill Adolf Eichmann".'

Victor was aware that he would be asked what alternative he proposed to a sentence of death. He gave what still seems to me a very weak reply. 'To answer this is no part of my purpose.'

He and I did a good deal of work together in penal reform. He showed (to my certain knowledge) a quite extraordinary degree of kindness to several individual prisoners but I do not think that at the end of his life he faced the problem of what to do about serious criminals. Any orthodox treatment of them came to seem a derogation from their God-given personality. One cannot think of him as any kind of Home Office Minister but his total influence for good was hardly diminished on the plane of action.

THE NON-FORGIVING MAN
PRIMO LEVI

It would be a mistake to assume that forgiveness is looked upon as a virtue by all men of intelligence or otherwise. Certainly there are many who would say that some things they can forgive and feel they ought to but some things they cannot. And in any case feel they ought not to. Those who have been injured and still more those whose loved ones have been injured or killed take pride not infrequently in saying that never under any circumstances will they forgive the wrongdoers. Myself, as a friend of some well-known prisoners, I am no stranger to this reaction. From a rather different point of view a very successful newspaper columnist, Janet Street-Porter, warned her readers about the dangers of too-ready forgiveness. In her view it bottled up resentments with disastrous psychological results. She insisted (contrary I am sure to the fact) that the forgiveness expressed by Mr Wilson of Enniskillen had brought about a nervous breakdown. His shattering experience combined with the loss of his daughter was surely sufficient in itself. No professed Christian could possibly accept Miss Street-Porter's advice, but I must assume that she understands her own wide public.

Primo Levi, a writer who was for many years admired on all sides, committed suicide in 1987. His posthumous work *The Drowned and the Saved* has been highly praised. Paul Bailey, a prominent critic, ends his introduction in this way: 'Primo Levi seems to me to be one of that select band of writers with whom it is possible to sustain a lasting friendship. One can turn to him for advice and help. He has a hard-won wisdom, and that wisdom will ensure his survival. He kept faith, in his faithfulness. His books offer us what Geoffrey Grigson detected in the best poetry of W. H. Auden "Explicit recipes for being human".' I should mention that just previously, Bailey had congratulated Levi for refusing 'to seek refuge in prayer even when his end seemed imminent'.

Levi, an Italian Jew, presents himself in his writings as the essential non-believer. From that point of view, it was no doubt more honest to maintain his unbelief to the end. What, however, is relevant to our purpose is the unforgivingness of this brilliant man described by many as a genius. The following two passages bring out his total refusal to adopt a forgiving attitude:

> 'That I do not feel hatred against the German surprises many, and it should not. In reality, I do not understand

> hatred, but only *ad personem*. If I were a judge, even though repressing what hatred I might feel, I would not hesitate to inflict the most severe punishment or even death on the many culprits who still today live undisturbed on German soil or in any other countries of suspect hospitality; but I would experience horror if a single innocent were punished for a crime he did not commit.'

In other words the innocent should not be punished, but there could be no forgiveness for the guilty to the end of time.

Throughout this book and his other writings, he comes back again and again to his passionate desire to *understand* the torturers. He tries to make allowances for their circumstances but feels bound to end with a biting denunciation of the German people.

> 'Let it be clear that to a greater or lesser degree all were responsible. But it must be just as clear that behind their responsibility stands that great majority of Germans, who accepted in the beginning, out of mental laziness myopic calculations, stupidity and national pride, the "beautiful words" of Corporal Hitler, followed him as long as luck and the lack of scruples favoured him, were swept away by his ruin, afflicted by deaths, misery and remorse, and rehabilitated a few years later as the result of an unprincipled political game.'

The reasons for his suicide will always remain mysterious but it seems possible to speculate that if he had been able to turn his undying hatred into something closer to human sympathy he would be alive today. But then, he would have been a very different man and the world might have been deprived of some memorable books.

CHAPTER FOUR

Forgiveness in literature

SHAKESPEARE

It is an obvious duty to seek forgiveness in Shakespeare, the more so as Charles Williams wrote a remarkable chapter under that heading in his book *The Forgiveness of Sin*. It was first published in 1942 and dedicated to the Inklings who are usually associated with the circle of C. S. Lewis. Williams concentrated on two plays in particular 'Measure for Measure' and 'Cymbeline'. 'In the tragedies the question of forgiveness does not arise. It may be said that that is one reason why they are tragedies. The hesitation to regard oneself as wronged, the capacity not to brood over wrong – this itself is lacking in Hamlet and Othello. It is a personal grudge, indulged, which distracts both of them. The wrongs of Lear are lost in madness; the sins of Macbeth are offered no chance of pardon.'

In 'Measure for Measure' Angelo on becoming the Acting Governor of Verona condemns a young man named Claudio to death for having intercourse with a girl before marriage. Isabella, Claudio's sister, novice of St Clare, appeals to Angelo for her brother's pardon. He falls in love with her and offers her the pardon in exchange for her consent to his lust. By a trick, his earlier pledged love to Mariana is substituted for Isabella. But when the night is ended, Angelo orders Claudio to be executed. All is discovered when the Duke of Verona returns. Angelo now begs the Duke:

> Then, good prince,
> No longer session hold upon my shame,
> But let my trial be my own confession.
> Immediate sentence then and sequent death
> Is all the grace I beg.

Isabella, at the last minute, kneels before the Duke and pleads for his pardon

> Most bounteous sir,
> Look, if it please you, on this man
> condemned . . .

The pardon is duly granted

Williams, though open-minded on the question of whether Shakespeare was or was not a Christian, considers this a near-perfect example of forgiveness. 'He who has caused the wrong, asked for his punishment; he who has suffered is asked for pardon.'

But he finds a still nobler more inspiring example of forgiveness in 'Cymbeline'. The noblest of Shakespeare's women, Imogen, has been condemned by her husband Posthumus to death for (as he thinks) disloyalty. She supposes him to be in love with someone else, and to desire her death, and she rebukes him to herself with the phrase;

> My dear Lord,
> Thou art one of the false ones.

The husband, Posthumus, exhibits a 'passion of repentance'. In William's words 'he is so far worthy of and prepared for her forgiveness'. Forgiveness all round takes over. The king finally pronounces: 'Pardon the word to all'.

Williams finds the theme of pardon more expressed in

'Cymbeline' than in any of the other plays. 'Pardon', he says in 'Cymbeline' seems almost to create the love to which it responds. His own conclusion is expressed near the end of his book. 'The mutual act of forgiveness is a holy thing: the proper disposition towards it, accepted or not accepted, remains holy.' We have passed at this point beyond the simple duty of forgiving someone who has wronged us, whether the word forgiveness is still the correct one is a matter of semantics. Williams still maintaining an agnosticism about Shakespeare's religion, suggests that he was sufficiently inspired to arrive at a religious conclusion.

DOSTOEVSKY
Crime and Punishment

More than one good judge of literature has told me that if I am writing about forgiveness I must not fail to deal with Dostoevsky. *Crime and Punishment* seems the favoured model. It has been a pleasure to re-read that tremendous story. (Incidentally, Ian Brady, convicted of the terrible Moors murders, whom I have visited in prison and more recently in a mental hospital for twenty years, has told me that *Crime and Punishment* is his favourite book.) For a long time *Crime and Punishment* does not seem to be bringing in forgiveness. But towards the end it figures strongly. The murderer of two old women, Rashkolnikov, is forgiven by the divinely generous Sonia who follows him when he is sent to Siberia. After much agonizing he begins to tell her the truth about the murder.

> 'Have you guessed?' he whispered at last.
>
> 'Oh God!' a terrible wail broke from her bosom. She sank helplessly on the bed, her face buried in the pillows. But a moment later she sat up quickly, moved rapidly towards him, seized his hands and clasping them tightly, as though in a vice, in her thin fingers, stared motionless-

ly at him, her eyes glued to his face. . . . Suddenly as though cut to heart she gave a start, uttered a cry, and, not knowing herself why, threw herself on her knees before him.

'Oh, what have you done to yourself?' she cried in despair and, jumping up, she flung herself on his neck, and held him tightly in her arms.'

'So you won't leave me, Sonia, will you?' he said, looking at her almost with hope.

'No, no – never – never!' Sonia exclaimed, 'I'll go with you everywhere! Oh, God! Oh, I'm so miserable! And why, why didn't I know you before? Why didn't you come to me before? Dear God!'

'Well, I've come now.'

But that is not the whole of her reaction.

He asks her 'What am I to do now?'

'What are you to do?' she cried, suddenly jumping to her feet and her eyes, which had been full of tears, flashed fire. 'Get up!'

She seized him by the shoulder, and he raised himself, looking at her almost in astonishment.

'Go at once, this very minute, and stand at the crossroads, bow down to all the four corners of the world – and say to all men aloud, "I am a murderer!" The God will send you life again. Will you go? Will you?' she asked him, trembling all over, seizing his hands and clasping them tightly in hers and looking at him with burning eyes.

He goes to the police. He is duly convicted though some unselfish actions of his are remembered in his favour. The book moves to Siberia.

For a long time Rashkolnikov seemed to deteriorate in Siberia. He is unpleasant to Sonia and gets himself thoroughly disliked by his fellow-prisoners. He cannot bring himself to repent.

> 'And if fate had only sent him repentance – burning repentance that would have rent his heart and deprived him of sleep - the sort of repentance that is accompanied by terrible agony which makes one long for the noose or the river! Oh, how happy he would have been if he could have felt such repentance! Agony and tears – why, that, too, was life! But he did not repent of his crime.'

Then he underwent a traumatic experience. Sonia was taken ill. He was very upset and sent to enquire after her. On learning, in turn, that Rashkolnikov was so upset and worried about her, Sonia sent him a pencilled note, telling him that she was much better and that she hoped to come and see him at his work very soon. His heart beat fast when he read that note. When they met:

> 'Suddenly something seemed to seize him and throw him at her feet. He embraced her knees and wept. . . . '

The book ends with Dostoevsky pointing the way forward 'to the gradual rebirth of a man, to his gradual re-generation, to his gradual passing from one world to another, to his acquaintance to new and hitherto unknown reality.'

Is there a central message here which is relevant to forgiveness. Only this perhaps, that where real love is present, as in the heart of Sonia, forgiveness is extended automatically, but where it is allied to spiritual inspiration it can bring about the repentance and re-generation of the sinner.

THOMAS HARDY
Tess of the d'Urbervilles

Hardy's *Tess of the d'Urbervilles* is another book which it seems to be agreed must be dealt with by any writer on forgiveness. Tess is one of the best-loved characters in fiction, though she was seduced early on and in the end was hanged for murdering her seducer. She is certainly a more memorable character than Trollope's Alice, though Sonia in *Crime and Punishment* has higher claim to sanctity.

There is a great deal in *Tess of the d'Urbervilles* about forgiveness, although Hardy, a stark agnostic, would seem to have little interest in the Christian view of that virtue. After her unfortunate start, Tess gets married to the rather stuffy son of a local clergyman, that is to say, well above her station. There comes a moment when he confides to her a sexual indiscretion of his own, whereupon she tells him with relief of her seduction. The reactions of the two, however, are very different. Angel Clare had told her of that time in his life when, tossed about by doubts and difficulties in London, like a cork on the waves, he plunged into eight-and-forty hours' dissipation with a stranger.

'Happily I awoke immediately to a sense of my folly' he continued. 'I would have no more to say to her, and I came home. I have never repeated the offence. But I felt I should like to treat you with perfect frankness and honour, and I could not do without telling this. Do you forgive me?'

Her reply was enthusiastic. 'Oh, Angel, I am almost glad, because you can forgive *me*. I have not made my confession, too, remember, I said so.'

But when she tells him her story, his response is horrifyingly different. 'Am I to believe this? From your manner I am to take it as true. O you cannot be out of your mind? You ought to be! Yet you are not . . . My wife, my Tess – nothing in you warrants such a supposition as that? . . . '

Sickly white, she jumped up. 'I thought, Angel, that you loved me – me, my very self? If it is I you do love, O how can it be that you look and speak so? It frightens me! Having begun to love you, I love you for ever – in all changes, in all disgraces, because you are yourself. I ask no more. Then how can you, O my husband, stop loving me?'

Angel replies: 'I repeat, the woman I have been loving is not you.'

'But who?'

'Another woman in your shape'.

He rejects her totally and appears to have passed out of her life. Desperate to find some way of providing for her family, she resumes contact with the seducer. Then Angel returns in the hope of her forgiving him. What had happened in the meanwhile, she describes in agonized terms.

'Angel', she said, 'do you know what I have been running after you for? To tell you that I have killed him. . . . I have done it – I don't know how. Still I owe it to you and to myself. Why did you go away, why did you, when I loved you so? I can't think why you did it. But I don't blame you only Angel, will you forgive me my sin against you, now I have killed him? I thought as I ran along that you would be sure to forgive me now I have done that. It came to me as a shining light that I should get you back that way. I could not bear the loss of you any longer – you don't know how entirely I was unable to bear your not loving me! Say you do now, dear dear husband, say you do, now I have killed him!

'I do love you, Tess, Oh, I do – it is all coming back!' he said, tightening his arms round her with fervid pressure. 'But how do you mean – you have killed him?' Clare asks her, 'Is he dead?'

'Yes', she replied. 'He heard me crying about you, and he bitterly taunted me, and called you by a foul name; and then I did it. My heart could not bear it. He had nagged me about you before. And then I dressed myself and came away to find you.'

Tess and Angel have a few unforgettable days together on the run. Then she wakes from sleep as a number of men close in on them.

'What is it, Angel?' she said, starting up. 'Have they come for me?'

'Yes, dearest,' he said, 'they have come.'

'It is as it should be,' she murmured. 'Angel, I am almost glad – yes, glad! This happiness could not have lasted. It was too much. I have had enough; and now I shall not live for you to despise me!'

She stood up, shook herself, and went forward, neither of the men having moved. 'I am ready' she said quietly.

The book ends with Angel Clare and Tess's sister watching the black flag being raised over the prison to signify the execution of Tess. Justice, says Hardy, was done, and the President of the Immortals, in Aeschylean phrase, had ended his sport with Tess. The sub-title describes Tess as a pure woman, the outcry at the time is perhaps understandable. Hardy, apart from telling a great story, is no doubt indicting a number of Victorian values. His theory of forgiveness, if any, would have no connection with Christianity. But the book makes out, none the less, a powerful case for forgiveness as generally understood. Angel Clare's failure to forgive Tess in the first place led on to tragedy. His forgiving her for a much more serious offence came too late to save her life, but not too late to bring them together at the end. Tess readily forgives Clare at all times. She cannot forgive her wicked seducer. Nevertheless Hardy's claim that she was a pure woman will be accepted by most of us always.

ANTHONY TROLLOPE
Can you forgive her?

Anthony Trollope's *Can you Forgive Her?* sounds promising for our purpose, though it does not carry us very far forward. The question 'Can You Forgive Her?' is posed by Trollope to the reader in the thirty-seventh chapter. The She in question is Alice Bavasor who broke off an engagement to the worthy but rather dull John Grey and became engaged to a typical cad, her cousin, George Bavasor.

Eventually she returns to Grey and accepts the prospect of a subordinate role in marriage. Trollope poses the question for the first time in this way. She knew that she could not forgive herself. 'But can you forgive her, delicate reader? Or am I asking the question too early in my story? For myself, I have forgiven her. The story of the struggle has been present to my mind for many years – and I have learned to think that even this offence against womanhood may, with deep repentance, be forgiven. And you also must forgive her before we close the book, or else my story will have been told amiss.' Much further on, in Chapter Seventy, he answers the question somewhat differently. 'Oh, reader, can you forgive her in that she sinned against the softness of her feminine nature? I think that she may be forgiven, in that she had never brought herself to think lightly of her own fault.'

The last paragraph of the book provides a further submission. 'Probably my readers may agree with Alice, that in the final adjustment of her affairs she had received more than she had deserved. All her friends, except her husband, thought so. But as they have all forgiven her, including even Lady Midlothian herself, I hope that they who have followed her story to its close will not be less generous.'

What general view of forgiveness can we extract from Trollope bearing in mind that Trollope was a great narrative writer, not a theorist. Certainly he seems to be saying that we must repent if we expect to be forgiven, but in the second passage quoted above, he seems to be giving additional marks to Alice for realizing from the beginning that she was doing wrong. What is more interesting, perhaps, is the emphasis laid on her failure for a long time to forgive herself. John Grey is represented as a rather heavy-handed kind of man, but he seems to have possessed not only virtue but intuition. I think I can make her happy, he said, if she will marry me, but she must be taught to forgive herself. We are told towards the end that Alice 'had not forgiven herself, would never forgive herself altogether'. But we are left with the impression that John Grey in his masterful fashion will bring this about in the end.

CHAPTER FIVE

Forgiveness and politics

For a number of years a valuable project has been carried out under the heading, 'Politics and Forgiveness'. Mr Frost, the Director, provides the flavour.

Mr Frost writes: 'forgiveness can perhaps best be seen as a way of dealing with wrong so that the past does not prevent a different future from being created.' He continues: 'Politics can be understood as that process whereby human beings organise their life together and apportion out the inevitable pain which we must all experience as we live in community in a world of limited resources.'

So far so good, though others might use other phrases to say the same thing. What follows is more controversial. He asks: '*How is the concept of corporate forgiveness related to change, history, repentance and conflict.*' There is an assumption here which I am ready to share but others may not. The concept of *corporate forgiveness* may seem (a) possible, (b) morally obligatory. But what of the argument widely used (though I do not accept it) that only (a) God and, (b) only the immediate victim are entitled to forgive. If that argument is accepted there cannot, of course, be any corporate forgiveness and the work of the Forgiveness and Politics Study project would be otiose from the beginning.

Mr Frost is no doubt familiar with the prolonged correspondence in *The Times* in 1985 and various subsequent exchanges about the duty of Jews to forgive the Germans collectively for the Holocaust. The point of view expressed by the Jewish writers seemed hostile to the whole idea of corporate forgiveness. Where that idea was entertained at all there seemed to be a demand that repentance should take place first. How this would ever be measured I have no idea.

As already mentioned, I myself was Minister for the British Zone of Germany from 1947 to 1948. The finest Christian minds in Britain (though not on the whole the leading politicians) were ready to forgive the Germans before they had had the chance to prove their penitence.

To focus discussion I will concentrate on some passages in the writings of a Mr Wilmer in the pamphlet 'Politics and Forgiveness' (April 1987). He attempts to eliminate 'the disagreeableness in politics'. 'I believe,' he writes, 'that the clue comes FROM THE HEART OF THE GOSPEL. The key word that means most to me is FORGIVENESS. But "forgiveness" is just one of a family of words which point in the same direction and if you prefer another word it does not matter. It is the reality rather than a particular word that counts.'

Is Mr Wilmer now passing beyond the definition of forgiveness applied by Mr Frost? Is he broadening the concept so that it passes into the general idea of reconciliation between the groups and a general promotion of peace and harmony between them? I am not, of course, denying the enormous value of such studies but how far does it come under the heading of forgiveness? Has the concept been changed from a special way of handling the past into a contemporary day-to-day tolerance and understanding between individuals and communities?

Where does Mr Wilmer stand on the crucial issue of whether forgiveness should wait on repentance? I am assuming that he considers that it should be extended in advance of repentance, for example, to Germany after World War II, but I am not certain. I have studied very carefully what Mr Wilmer has to say about forgiveness and justice and punishment.

> 'It is a failure in historic Christianity that it has not understood its faith well enough to resist more strongly the tendency to treat forgiveness and justice as mutually contradictory, as though forgiveness meant an escape from justice. Whether it is seen as giving each man his due or as what is revealed in God's good will and deed in creating and redeeming the world, forgiveness is the very heart of justice. To forgive is just. Nor is it soft: the reason why forgiveness has been belittled is not because it is easy but because it is hard.'

I am hopeful that he means the same as I do when I say that punishment should ideally be administered in a spirit of love and, that at the very least, emotional hostility should be absent from the penal arrangements. To say as he does, 'to forgive is just' seems to me to be going too far but it may be only a matter of words. I do not, however, like his emphasis on forgiveness being hard.

Lord Hylton has spoken up more bravely and perceptively about forgiveness than anyone else in public life during the last few years. He has made a series of notable speeches in the House of Lords on the subject and made a public plea to Mrs Thatcher that she should initiate a dialogue of forgiveness between Britain and Ireland. No-one can doubt the value of such a dialogue if it ever occurred. But Lord Hylton is a little innocent, perhaps, in supposing that the people of Ireland will ever see anything to apologize for in events such as the Rising of 1916.

Many valuable papers have been prepared for the Forgiveness and Politics project in addition to those just mentioned. I can only touch on a few. The Rev. John Morrow has a special claim on our attention as the leader of the Corrymeela Community, the splendid ecumenical centre in Northern Ireland. In his paper prepared for this project he deals with practical policies rather than the religious or philosophical meaning of forgiveness. He lays much stress on the need for a coming together of the churches in England and Ireland. 'But it will only be a genuine pilgrimage if we are all moving towards a deeper discernment of Christ himself.' No-one can quarrel with him there.

One is bound to express doubts when he points towards new political arrangements in which it would seem to Irish people that their independence would be lost in a wider grouping. But his conclusion must carry everyone with it. 'Perhaps one way to move in this direction is to turn outwards to those who are and remain the worst victims of our divisions: the prisoners; the bereaved; the unemployed; the homeless; the orphans; the one-parent families; the embittered; the cynical; the despairing, and all trapped in fears real or imaginary. The call to reconciliation is always in the context of mission – our common mission to all people.'

Mrs Una O'Higgins O'Malley, President of the Irish Association for Cultural, Economic and Social Relations comes to grips more explicitly with the concept of forgiveness. Her father, Kevin O'Higgins, was assassinated in 1927 on his way to mass. He was Minister for Justice and Vice-President of the Executive Council which earlier had executed members of the armed forces opposed to that Government. She admits that there will be many in Ireland who will be slow to associate her father with forgiveness. But she reminds us of his dying words of forgiveness and compassion for those who had killed him. She considers it more than possible that if he lived he, a supreme realist, would have asked himself new questions.

Why, she asks, is Ireland still witnessing violence? Which (in her words) the repressive measures of successive governments did not appear to have yet quelled. 'The only way', she continues, 'to deal with the unforgiveable is to forgive it.'

Her practical message seems to be her demand for an enlightened penal policy based as never before on forgiveness. But as we keep finding in the present study, it is easier to demand such a policy than to work it out in practice.

The Rt Hon. David Bleakley, General Secretary of the Irish Council of Churches has himself a distinguished political record. He concerns himself here with a new federal grouping which would include Ireland, England, Scotland, and Wales. I cannot pretend that I see much possibility of that being established. The difference in size and strength between England and Ireland will always make it unpalatable to the latter quite apart from any British objections. Another suggestion of David Bleakley seems at first sight equally removed from reality. He hopes that of the celebrations in 1990 of the 300th anniversary of the Battle of the Boyne there may come a new readiness on the part of Irishmen to combine their positions. I would be inclined to discount this possibility as much as the other one he suggests, except for a personal experience. Two years ago I attended a memorable meeting at the Boyne organized by the Ulster Policewomen. Large parties came together from North and South. I shall never forget the emotion evoked by one of the Protestant speakers from the North when she cried aloud, 'No-one won a victory at the Boyne.' Hardly perhaps correct history, but if Bleakley had been there he might have pointed to it as the kind of reconciliation he is suggesting.

It is a long step to the next essayist, a young ex-member of the IRA who spent fifty-seven days on hunger strike. He only abandoned it when almost totally blind and told that his mother would take him off hunger strike when he passed into a coma. He had already been touched by a new religious belief. As he recovered from the hunger strike one incident stood out. Three ex-hunger strikers laughing at the death of a policeman killed in London and of people in a pub in England who laughed at the report of the death of a hunger striker. 'People everywhere are very much the same: gloating over deaths of the enemy and grieving over their own, never stopping to consider that their enemy had loved ones too. Jesus says, "Love your enemies, do good to them who hate you, bless those who curse you, pray for them who treat you badly." From that moment he was committed to Christ. He left that prison and in the new prison severed his connections with Republicanism. An Ex-member of the IRA also touched by Jesus Christ said to him when they were speaking about the Protestant and Catholic churches: 'The Church of God is like a swallow, two tails coming from different directions into one body with one head.'

Professor Enda McDonagh, a Professor at Maynooth Seminary in Co. Kildare in the Irish Republic, reminds us that the world left by Christ was to be 'a world shaped by forgiveness.' And yet he went on, 'We live for the most part in an unforgiving and unforgiven world. It is time', he concluded, 'for the British and Irish, the Protestants and the Catholics, to take up the message of Jesus Christ when he said to the paralytic, "Your sins are forgiven you." Forgive one another. In that fashion we might hope to overcome our national and international paralysis. We might hope to take up our pallets, we might hope to set one another free in the forgiveness of Jesus Christ.'

Bishop Cahal B. Daly of Down and Connor, has at the time of writing achieved a position of exceptional repute in Britain and Ireland. Once again, as often before and since, he condemns violence and condemns it in terms which would mean much to every Irishman. 'I have no doubt but that Padraig Pearse would long ago have called off the campaign (of violence), as he did on the Saturday of Easter Week, 1916, "in order to prevent further slaughter of citizens".' He points with horror to some of the more awful deeds committed by the IRA in the name of Irish patriotism, but he insists that 'peace can only come through justice . . . .' It is time to face squarely the fact that justice requires new political institutions in Northern

Ireland. And here the appeal must be made to the British Government, seeing that it was 'the British who devised and imposed the faulty constitution fron which our present problems ultimately stem.'

He does not take it on himself to explain the nature of the reforms he has in mind, but reforms there must be if personal reconciliation is to be made possible. His last word, however, takes the form of a quotation from Pope John Paul II: 'The message that I send to you is both simple and demanding, for it concerns each of you personally. It invites each one to do his or her share in the establishment of peace (in our society) without passing this duty on to others.' So he's appealing alike to governments, parties, and individual men and women.

I will round off this chapter with two quotations from Bishop Daly of Down and Connor. They are taken from a homily delivered by him at the funeral masses of three Catholic victims of the 'Avenue Bar' shooting on Wednesday, 18 May 1988. Most of the homily dwelt on the victims, but these two passages were especially notable: 'All three bereaved families and all the five injured whom I have seen in hospital are at one in their spirit of forgiveness and in asking that there be no retaliation. All have seen from bitter experience the utter evil and the total senselessness of all killing and they want to see no more of it. I believe that this is the conviction of the immense majority of people in both the Catholic and the Protestant communities.'

Earlier in the sermon he had spoken out still more bluntly. 'We pray at all of today's funerals for the perpetrators of all these murders. May God in His great mercy forgive them and grant them the grace to repent of their sins, to be freed from their murdering hate, to be forgiven by God and to change their lives. We make our own the prayer of Christ on the Cross for his executioners: "Father, forgive them, for they do not know what they are doing".' (Luke 23:34)

At that point some members of the congregation walked out. It is said that they had gone there with that intention, but I have no means of knowing whether that is so.

CHAPTER SIX

Forgiveness in Northern Ireland

The previous chapter was based on what I had read. This one is derived from personal encounters.

Friday, 3 June 1988 I spent in Belfast. Apart from discussions with clergy and others, I interviewed five people (four of them women) who had suffered grievously through assassination. Three of them had had their husbands murdered, one had lost his son and had been nearly killed himself, when his car was riddled with eleven bullets; another woman had been seized coming out of church and tied up while in the darkness she could hear her companion being shot. The next day, Saturday, a kindly teacher and his wife, a headmistress, Anne Tammey, who had arranged the Friday interviews, drove me to Enniskillen.

There I interviewed Mr Gordon Wilson who has achieved world fame, much against his will, through the message he delivered on television after his daughter's murder on 8 November 1987 in the Enniskillen bombing and his own narrow escape from death.

'I was pushed forward on my face', he said, 'when the bomb went off. The rubble and the wall and the railings fell on top of us. I then felt someone holding my hand. It was Marie. When I asked her the fifth time if she was all right she said, "Daddy, I love you very much". Those were her last words.'

Mr Wilson told me that these words filled him with inexpressible love. In his television talk he continued, 'My wife, Joan (she had incidentally done much to bring Catholic and Protestant children together at musical weekends) and I do not bear any grudges. We do not hold any ill-will against those responsible for this. We see it as God's plan, even though we might not understand it. I shall pray for those people tonight and every night. God forgive them, for they know not what they do.' He added this: 'All I know is that we have lost a gorgeous girl.' On that everyone was agreed.

Marie had won the Duke of Edinburgh's Gold Award. Her certificate shows that she did community service, made a foot expedition in the Sperrins mountain range of County Tyrone, sang, did judo, and took a youth orchestra course at Sterling University.

She received her award from Prince Philip at St James's Palace in June 1987.

Mr Wilson's words were carried far and wide. He himself received many thousands of letters. After fifteen thousand they stopped counting. The Clerk of the Enniskillen Council told me that three hundred thousand letters had come to them. The Queen made Mr Wilson's forgiveness the basis of her Christmas message. He told me that when he went to a hotel in Dublin, twenty-four out of the twenty-five diners came across to shake his hand.

Gordon Wilson is an impressive man to meet. He presides over a large shop in the main street of the town. He prides himself on being an ordinary draper, but he must at least concede that he is a very successful one. He is well over six feet in height (his son is still taller), lean, bespectacled, well accustomed to welcoming customers whether Protestants or Catholics or neither. I told him that I had started life as a member of the Church of Ireland, but had now been for many years a Roman Catholic. He asked me, twinkling, 'Why not try Methodism?' of which he is a local pillar.

I had heard that he had had something of a breakdown after the tragedy of his daughter's death, his own injuries – some of them permanent, and his emergence as a reluctant hero. If so, he showed no sign of it. But he talked frankly about the psychological consequences. The real threat to his happiness were the media, about whom he spoke with underlying apprehension. He had visited a psychiatrist at one point when his claim was being drawn up for personal damage. The psychiatrist told him that his grief for his much-loved daughter would never disappear, but the traumatic effects of the episode would fade gradually. He must, however, expect considerable distress on the anniversary of 8 November 1987. What appalled him was the thought that the media would concentrate, like ghouls, on his bearing on that occasion. However, he had Christian faith and belief that he would come through. The depth of his sorrow was hinted when he disclosed in passing that he and his wife had not yet felt able to visit the grave *together* for fear of breaking down.

Which leads me on to a remarkable fact about Gordon Wilson. Everyone that I have known who has experienced much publicity has only complained of it when it was adverse, or at least unsatisfactory. No-one could have had 'a better press' than Gordon Wilson, but he was horrified by the effect that he thought it was having on him. When in London he had been given lunch by Neil Kinnock, Leader of the Opposition, and Kevin Macnamara, Shadow Minister for Northern Ireland. He asked them, 'When will I get back to being the Gordon Wilson I was before the tragedy?' They both told him, 'You never will.'

What he had to say about his reasons for expressing forgiveness was very simple. It never occurred to him to say or do anything else, although out of many favourable letters, one correspondent suggested that he must have been drugged. He had said the Lord's Prayer all his life. It was instinctive to act accordingly. 'Forgive us our trespasses,' he quoted to me ('as we forgive them that trespass against us'). He might have quoted, in view of what he said on television, 'Love your enemies, pray for those that persecute you.' He brought home to me, as never before, that forgiveness is or should be a positive quality not just a rejection of bitterness. After all, praying for someone is an act of love. A humanist can no doubt eliminate his bitterness for various reasons, but he is unlikely to believe in the efficacy of prayer.

One result of my talks with Gordon Wilson and those I met on the previous day is to confirm me in the conviction that forgiveness represents a particularly Christian virtue. No doubt, as indicated above, there are sound psychological reasons for refusing to allow bitterness and still more hatred to accumulate in one's heart. President Nixon when he resigned from the Presidency, announced that he would not allow himself to be destroyed by such feelings. He had had, as it happened, a Quaker upbringing, but in any case his approach was psychologically sound. I am not suggesting therefore that no-one who is not a Christian can forgive. But I am more sure than ever after talks just referred to that instinctive forgiveness is much more likely in a Christian who has had for many years the model of Christ to live up to.

Not that it is invariable. Anne Tammey tells me that the kind of people who are ready to talk about forgiveness are not typical. They are those who found it possible to forgive. This would not be true of all their neighbours. There was a lady whose husband had been murdered most brutally and had agreed to see me. But when we called, she did not feel up to it. One of the ladies we talked to told me that she had had no difficulty in forgiving the men who killed her husband. But it may be that her recollection was at fault. She had admitted some time earlier to finding forgiveness most difficult, but by prayer and through Holy Communion she had reached a state of mind in which her earlier bitterness was best forgotten.

One lady would not, I think, claim that forgiveness was her reaction, though she is a good woman and no doubt a Christian. I stayed with her and her husband twice while I was preparing to speak in the House of Lords on the Supergrass system. Later her husband was assassinated by the IRA while she and her children were in the house. He was accused of paramilitary activities, which I need not go into now.

Her eleven-year-old son was present when I called on this occasion. It would have been ludicrous to expect him to forgive the men who had murdered his father. His mother was tight-lipped. She did not spend time on saying what she no doubt thought about the IRA. She and her husband had no doubt long regarded them as the enemy. I know from talking to members of that body in prison that they regard atrocious acts of violence as acts of war. No doubt the Protestant paramilitaries feel the same. My friend, the widow, was more concerned to castigate the police for their failure to save her husband's life when he lay badly wounded. I have noticed that those who have suffered greatly from atrocities by unknown assailants tend to reserve their extreme animosity for known individuals.

My impression is that those who in Northern Ireland have suffered from horrible atrocities are not usually anxious to identify those who have done the evil thing. They are no more anxious perhaps than were those who suffered similar afflictions during the blitz to identify the pilot who dropped the fatal bombs. No doubt there is an infinite variety of reactions. The woman, already mentioned, who was tied up while her companion was shot in the darkness was obsessed with the desire to find the man who had tied her up. He had spoken nicely and said, 'I am sorry to have to do this'. She could only hope to discover the man through his voice. It was too dark to see his face. The obsession passed away. She could not now understand it and bore no ill-will against the man. She just entertained this strange curiosity.

But to repeat myself, it is the known individual whether

or not the architect of the crime who may create a lasting resentment. Even Gordon Wilson, so completely Christian, was aware of this difficulty. He discussed with us at length the problem of how he should behave, if and when he encountered the Chairman of the Enniskillen Council, who it should be explained is a representative of Sinn Fein, the admitted political wing of the IRA. The latter organization had taken responsibility for the bomb massacre in which so many lost their lives. Their leader, Gerry Adams, expressed on television regret for the civilian deaths. The Chairman of the Council, although he said something in public to the same effect, refrained from expressing any direct sympathy to Gordon Wilson or his family.

What would the forgiving man, that is to say, Gordon Wilson, say or do when he met the Chairman? Suppose, for example, that the Chairman actually called on him. Anne Tammey and I offered fairly conventional advice. Gordon Wilson remained uncertain. (Did loyalty to his beloved daughter come in here?) He said finally that he hoped and prayed that he would receive the same guidance as when he spoke after the tragedy.

Gordon Wilson, once more with delightful frankness, discussed the problem of his personal role in times ahead. He was being invited to lecture everywhere, at home and abroad; to be the champion of the values which he had expressed with such tremendous impact on television. I told him that anyone who wrote on forgiveness, who like myself have not suffered grave injury, must always look to him for a wider leadership. But after talking to his friends, he was convinced that this role was not for him. He was a *draper* and he would be embarking on a course of action that God had not intended for him if he attempted to become a spiritual propagandist. Yet he realized that he could not simply fold his hands and put the whole thing away from him. After further discussion I suggested that he should attempt a memoire of his daughter. Speaking as a hardened autobiographer, I felt that autobiography was too egocentric for him.

Martin Wright, former Director of the Howard League, now Chief Information Officer of the organization National Association of Victims' Support Schemes (NAVSS) had told me the day before in England that some of the finest victims had felt a strong urge to make sure that some good came out of their personal tragedies.

My friend, Jane Ewart-Biggs, now Baroness Ewart-Biggs, is a shining example of this. Her husband was murdered just after becoming Ambassador to the Irish Republic. Within a few days she delivered a telling broadcast whose impact was comparable to that of Gordon Wilson. She dedicated herself to doing something for the people of Ireland.

She is the first to say that her motive was not connected with religion, nor could it be described at that moment as love of Ireland. She had only briefly visited the country, though she has acquired a strong affection for it since. What inspired her was a passionate desire to make sure that her husband's life was not wasted. He had been entertaining such high hopes for his mission to Ireland. She was going to be faithful to his memory by carrying on what would have been his work. Since then she has nobly lived up to her aspiration through the Ewart-Biggs Memorial Trust to do something *positive* to realize his dream.

On various levels this same determination that good should come out of evil has been present among many of the victims in Belfast, though I am not suggesting for a moment that it has been universal.

In most cases there was some 'getting together' of those who had suffered in this way. The eminent surgeon, Mr Gormley, was an example as striking as Mr Wilson, of forgiveness. His son, as already indicated, was murdered when his car was riddled with bullets. He himself escaped with his life, though severely injured. As he was being taken to hospital he exclaimed instinctively, 'Father, forgive them for they know not what they do.' Since then he has taken an initiative in starting a movement for peace with a group of Catholic and Protestant friends.

A Catholic priest whose social work brings him into close touch with both the religious communities, considers that there is, all things considered, a high level of forgiveness in Northern Ireland. Perhaps there is an acceptance of the fact that the evil that men do in the Province can be attributed for the most part to causes beyond the individual transgressor. In England where political crime is negligible and so-called ordinary crime rising steadily, the attitude of victims is likely to be different. Be that as it may a spirit of forgiveness is operating strongly in Northern Ireland under religious leadership. But always there remain the paramilitary bodies for whom forgiveness has no meaning and revenge all too much.

I will end by mentioning two women whom I did not meet in Northern Ireland but who reflect the spirit I found to be widely represented there.

In a small book Alf McCreary, an award-winning Belfast journalist, has collected some arresting examples of forgiveness under the title: *Profiles of Hope*. Two examples may be brought in here.

Dr Hylda Armstrong is a woman who has overcome great personal tragedy and has maintained a positive and creative attitude to life. Her husband died at thirty-eight from cancer, leaving her with two young boys. A much-loved niece was killed in a motor accident and she herself was badly injured in a traffic mishap. In 1973 her elder son Sean was shot dead in Belfast by an unknown gunman.

Sean carried out reconciliation work with children, and after his death Dr Armstrong became a founder member of Harmony Community Trust which has the express aim of enabling Protestant and Roman Catholic children to get to know one another better. 'Bitterness', she writes, 'eats away at people. I have never felt bitter, not even at the man who shot Sean. I don't know that I would ever want to meet him. But I would rather be the mother of Sean than the mother of the man who shot him. It must be dreadful to be the mother or the wife of someone who had done something terrible. That really is a harder cross to bear. You can lose someone and still love them, but if my son had been guilty of terrorism in any way I would like to think that I would still love him. But it would be terrible to think that a child of mine had treated another human being in that way.'

Mrs Maurer Kiely is a housewife whose teenage son was shot dead by an unknown gunman on the steps of a church in Belfast. She now runs the Cross Group for others who have lost a husband or relative as a result of the violence. 'There was no point', she writes, 'in saying the Lord's Prayer if I was not prepared to forgive. So I don't care if they never catch the boy who shot him. As a matter of fact I would prefer that they didn't. The police say: "He was probably your own son's age and he was probably given a five pound note for doing it! So he was sent out . . ." I would hate to see him being caught and sent to prison for thirty years and in one way to rot. But his conscience is bound to disturb him as he gets older. If they ever did catch him I would be prepared to meet that boy and if he wanted to talk I would be willing to forgive him, if he was genuinely sorry for what he had done. But I would never forget.'

So forgiveness, even among the finest spirits, remains a complicated process and in this world is not likely to be quite complete.

CHAPTER SEVEN

Victims in general

It seems proper in a book on forgiveness to touch, however briefly, on victims and their reaction to the atrocities that may be inflicted on them. My own concern with victims goes back some way. In 1964 I took the Chair of a Committee of Justice (the lawyers' society) to make proposals for better treatment for victims of crime. Subsequently I introduced a motion on that subject into the House of Lords. Not long afterwards, though I must not overestimate my influence, the scheme for Criminal Injuries Compensation was introduced.

Between 1977 and 1979 I was active again in the same cause. I initiated and took the Chair of a Committee concerned with Victims. Later I introduced a Private Member's Bill with the same purpose which made considerable headway. At that time the number of victim support schemes of any kind was very small. Now there are over 300 such schemes, undoubtedly proving of much consolation to victims.

The National Association of Victim Support Schemes is beginning to exert a real influence. Though the absence of a central body has hitherto made them, in political terms, a weak lobby, it has many offshoots. As I write I have in front of me the Annual Report of the Forum for Initiatives in Reparation and Mediation (FIRM). This was started in 1985 as a formal voluntary organization. It had grown out of an informal group of people involved in carrying out the planning for some of the earliest mediation projects between victims and offenders. Since then the group has widened its interest considerably to include all aspects of mediation in conflicts, not confined to criminal justice. In its own terms: 'The Forum exists to serve its members and to promote more constructive ways of settling conflicts, without violence, without fights, and without bitterness and rancour.'

How far does the concept of forgiveness enter into their philosophy or activities? There is certainly nothing specifically Christian in the UK literature. Some of those engaged describe themselves as Christians, some very definitely not. The same is true of the victims and offenders whom they seek to bring together.

The word forgiveness itself does not feature strongly, or at all. Nevertheless, those who have suffered injury and are reconciled to the wrongdoers in this way will probably reply, in most cases, 'Yes, I forgive them.' That is, supposing the question will be asked, which in most cases perhaps it would not be.

Repentance may be rather a highflown word to apply to the attitude of the typical offender who is ready to render an apology to his victim. But it can perhaps be legitimately used. Certainly the encounter between the victim and offender when it is brought about begins with a formal apology. But as the conversation proceeds and a relationship develops I am told that the apology becomes a good deal more heartfelt.

A little cynicism but not too much is permissible here. The offender who expresses himself ready to meet his victim and apologize to him is, in some cases at least, not yet sentenced. In other words, he can reasonably calculate that he will benefit from showing contrition. But in other cases he would have been sentenced already.

I am told that in about forty per cent of cases handled a personal encounter actually takes place between offender and victim, although sixty per cent of victims may have begun by saying that they were ready for a meeting. In a large number of other cases the victim is too distressed to want to meet the man who has done him wrong. Nevertheless mediation can take place without a personal encounter.

It must be understood that the driving force behind these schemes does not only come from an official view that the offender will be brought to appreciate the enormity of his crimes more effectively if he meets, or at any rate is made fully aware of the personality of, the victim, but there is also an official readiness to treat it as a means of reducing crime.

It is also claimed that the experience of meeting the offender, expressing feelings, asking questions and possibly being reconciled can be helpful to the victim in overcoming the psychological effects of the crime. There are, however, many crimes which are much more heinous. Increasingly, these too are dealt with through Victim Support Schemes. Inevitably where the offence has been murder the hostility to the wrongdoer is likely to be much greater.

Martin Wright, ex-Director of The Howard League has reviewed research into the rêaction of victims and criminals in the UK and USA. Victims, he has concluded, were not more punitive than non-victims.

'What they do want is that offenders should make some redress.' He himself has pressed unremittingly for a much greater emphasis on reparation and a much smaller emphasis on punishment in government policy. He insists with much evidence to back up his view that many people become less retributive in their attitude to criminals when more fully informed of the facts. In one particular case, he informs us, that when the public were informed of the background only 14.8 per cent of them thought the sentence too lenient and 44 per cent thought it was too harsh. 'Yet 90 per cent of the total sample had said, before the questions were put, that in general courts were too lenient. Another study was based on actual newspaper coverage of a case and on the court transcript. Of those who saw only the newspaper account, 63 per cent thought the sentence too lenient; but 53 per cent of those who saw the transcript thought it was too harsh.'

There is a general opinion that any referendum on capital punishment would favour a return to hanging. It may well be that the general public when asked the broad question would be governed by their feelings in regard to a whole number of sensationalized cases. If they were able to make a careful study of a number of these they might reach a different conclusion.

I cannot imagine any social investigation which would ever provide a simple answer to the question: how does the typical victim's relative respond to the typical murderer? The responses would, no doubt, be infinitely varied. In the Inquiry of my committee into victims, which I mentioned earlier, much of the inspiration came from Michael Whittaker whose daughter had been raped and murdered. He is one of many who, to my certain knowledge, have proved that it is at least possible, if terribly hard, to forgive a murderer in a truly Christian spirit.

Mediation, as I indicated earlier, is only one aspect of the extensive work of the Victim Support movement. Another is the NAVSS project for *families* of murder victims. On 26 February 1988 NAVSS announced a new national initiative offering support for the relatives of murder victims with allied research, designed to gain an understanding of their needs. It happened that two of the victims supported in this way were members with me of a panel in a television programme in June 1988, entitled, 'Survival after Murder'. One was a mother, one a father, each had lost through murder a dearly loved child. In the first case, the murderer had never been discovered. In the second case, he had been arrested and convicted, after a considerable interval, during which the father and others had undergone a horrible period of suspicion. All of us were moved by the poignant account of the event and its aftermath.

Both parents called for justice for the murderers, which clearly meant punishment at least as severe as they were likely to receive. The mother was apparently in favour of capital punishment; the father definitely not. He expressed alarm, however, that the murderer might be let out too soon and repeat his crime.

The panel showed much knowledgeable sympathy. I was the first, however, to raise the possibility of forgiveness. Some at least of my colleagues seemed to feel that I was being irrelevant. I recalled my recent visit to Northern Ireland described above and particularly my encounter with Gordon Wilson. The father whose child had been murdered acknowledged the nobility of Wilson's attitude, but seemed to feel that it could hardly be expected among ordinary people. Later I learnt that he had in fact worked hard among parents stricken like himself though he did not mention it at the time.

Subsequently I interviewed the man and woman running the NAVSS project. They insisted on the dangers of pushing forgiveness down people's throats. I told them that I had been shocked by an article by a popular female columnist which carried this point further. She insisted, for example, that Mr Wilson had suffered a nervous breakdown from 'forgiving too soon'. The directors of the project did not entirely agree with such a comment, quite apart from the fact that Mr Wilson had completely recovered. They brought home to me, however, the damaging effect of Press enquiries immediately after the murder. A grief-stricken parent is pressed to say immediately whether he or she does or does not forgive. An attitude is often assumed which is a liability later.

This is a book about 'Forgiveness' and not about techniques of healing or coping with distress. The directors of the project would certainly agree that forgiveness may have an important part to play in recovery. But one has to be very careful about insisting on it at the beginning. The great thing, they told me, is to listen and allow natural human feelings to work themselves out, even when those feelings are little more than those of anger and even hatred.

I told the directors that in Northern Ireland I had been warned that my examples were not representative. Those least likely to forgive were the least likely to talk to me. On the other hand, it might be that the more religious-minded of the relatives of the victims might be seeking consolation elsewhere.

It will be recognized that I have been taking extreme cases above. Murder is at one end of the scale; at the other lie the small annoyances which we encounter daily. The principle of forgiveness must be applied to each with due allowance for the difference in the suffering of the victim or the surviving relative.

No praise can be too high for the work of an organization such as that of the Compassionate Friends. 'An international organization of bereaved parents offering one another friendship and understanding'. They are concerned with bereaved parents of every kind. My wife and I who lost a much-loved daughter in a motoring accident twenty years ago would no doubt qualify. For our purpose their work for and among parents of murdered children is of special relevance. Anne Robinson whose son was brutally murdered subsequently started a group within the organization for the parents of murdered children. They have made splendid progress in the last few years.

Reading the admirable literature of the Compassionate Friends I do not easily find references to forgiveness. Religion is obviously handled with extreme caution. At one point, I read 'whilst religion and philosophical beliefs are . . . of benefit to some parents, the Compassionate Friends as an organization has no religious affiliation.'

I read elsewhere in an interview with two of the parents.

> Many of the parents have been to spiritualists. One said: 'You go for confirmation that there is life after death.' There are mixed feelings about religion. Mrs Margaret Buttle whose son was killed, said: 'Why did I bring up my kids in a Christian way, when this can happen?' Because of the strength of her feelings towards his assailants, she does not go to church anymore. She

cannot ask to have her trespasses forgiven as she would forgive those who have trespassed against her. 'I would feel a hypocrite'. she said.

The same kind of thing was said to me by the mother of the murdered child who took part with me in the television programme already mentioned.

Anne Robinson herself is an impressive woman. Her marriage was ultimately destroyed by the murder of her son. Her daughter, aged ten at the time, sadly admits that 'she never had a childhood'. The murder took place in Germany where Anne's husband was serving. It took eight years before the murderer was finally convicted of this and five other murders. Anne Robinson has not only returned to her career of nursing but she has founded this remarkable Fellowship of fellow sufferers.

She would not lay claim to a conscious religious motivation though she would describe herself as a Christian. She sometimes says the Lord's Prayer but today leaves out the passage about forgiveness. She feels that it would be hypocritical on her lips. She thinks of herself as a forgiving person but resolutely insists that a crime such as the murder of her son is unforgiveable. The same appears to be true of the great majority of the members of her Fellowship. She can only think of two who will say that at the present time they forgive the murderer.

I suggested to her that it was perhaps a sense of loyalty to the lost one that made forgiveness impossible. She said that two or three years ago that might have been true but not today; nor does she admit that in a general sense she has become bitter. But forgive she cannot and sees no prospect of doing so. No-one, she insists, who has not been through the experience can understand the agony caused at the time and the persisting consequences. I did not cross-examine her about her use of words. She is entitled to much sympathy and much respect.

Once again I am forced to the conclusion that forgiveness,

being so distinctive a Christian virtue, is more likely to occur if there is a Christian motivation in the healer or the man or woman to be healed. It is time to take a look at an attempt being made to combine a Christian and a psychological approach.

Work of exceptional interest is being performed by the Westminster Pastoral Foundation, originally a Methodist institution but now ecumenical. The Director is a Canon of the Church of England but also a fully-trained Jungian psychoanalyst. I conclude after a discussion with him that his inspiration is at once Christian and medical. Patients of all denominations or none, Christian or non-Christian, are welcomed. The language of forgiveness does not seem to be much employed but the Director left me in little doubt that if all goes well forgiveness should be the outcome of the treatment of victims.

The clientele is not, of course, confined to victims. Not only offenders but every sort of person is welcomed. The general message, however, has a special interest for us in our study of forgiveness.

A central purpose in the healing endeavour is to help people to face the facts about themselves and the nature of their feelings. It may be, therefore, that someone who announces that he forgives an offender will find, as he goes deeper, that he still retains feelings of bitterness. These have to be brought into the light of day before he can get rid of them. It is just as important that the patient or an offender should realize that he is himself forgiven. If he is a Christian this may well be brought home to him as the forgiveness of God. If not, the forgiveness of the analyst may be an effective substitute.

The Director called attention to a subtle difficulty which confronts a victim forgiving an offender. It is all too easy for him to forgive as it were from above, all too hard to place himself in some sense on the same level as the offender. But if he is properly humble, he will achieve this eventually. Forgiveness must be a process and if possible a mutual process.

The Vicar of Ealing, the Rev. Michael Saward, stands in many eyes on the same footing as Gordon Wilson as a supreme example of a forgiving man. His house was broken into by young men armed with knives. A young woman was raped. He and the young woman's boy friend were savagely beaten up. But at the end he was able to forgive his assailants. A year later (February 1987) he was able to write a main article in the *Sunday Telegraph* entitled 'Why I can forgive the men who did such evil'. His Christian spirit in the face of this appalling outrage is a magnificent example of what we look for from our religious leaders.

That said, sitting in my armchair seriously injured by no-one, I venture to disagree with some of his propositions. He says, for example:

> '*I cannot attempt to declare forgiveness on behalf of others*. If the rape victim is able to forgive then *she* must say so. It is empty and woolly-minded for me to think that I can do it for her. My response should be anger at those who raped her and a passionate concern for justice to be done to them by society's appointed arbitrators, the judges.'

A number of points seem to me to need sorting out here, some of which I have attempted to clarify in the body of this book and in the conclusions. Surely the first point to make is that we must distinguish the proper hatred for the crime from the duty of loving the criminal. I am horrified myself at the idea which is realized too often in practice that justice should be administered in a spirit of anger towards those who have committed a criminal offence.

But further, am I right in summarizing the Vicar's refusal to condemn his own assailants as due to a consciousness that we are all sinners and that none of us is qualified to cast the first stone? Does that not apply to society at least as much as to any individual?

His attitude to the appalling suffering of the Jews is far removed from mine, as will be seen from an earlier chapter. He says, 'I can say that what was done at Auschwitz diminishes all of us and that we ought to be passionately angry at the Western world's failure to deal adequately with the perpetrators of those outrages. Justice, which was loudly promised, was not done, then or since. However, I have no right to try to forgive on behalf of the Jewish people. They alone can do that if they wish.' But in what sense are the Jews of today able, on his argument, to forgive the Nazis, most of whom are dead or very old, let alone their descendants who cannot possibly be held responsible for their crimes. To accept that hopelessness would seem to be a counsel of despair.

CHAPTER EIGHT

Forgiveness and the criminal

I have already touched on this deep-rooted issue. It comes very close to my own experience. It is now fifty years since I began to visit men and women in prison. In the intervening period I have been involved on paper or in practice with almost every penal issue. In the early sixties I published a small book called *The Idea of Punishment*. It restated the four traditional elements in a just punishment. Deterrence, reform of the criminal, prevention (keeping him out of harm's way), and retribution, which I redefined as fairness. I expressed the hope that reparation would figure more largely. To a small extent that has happened in the last thirty years.

Since 1961 there has been a noticeable expansion of criminological studies, but this has been more than overtaken by the growing public animosity to criminals under the remorseless increase in crime. This public animosity, the precise opposite of forgiveness, has been exploited and augmented by the tabloid press. Where does forgiveness come into all this?

Let us take one aspect of our present penal system which is universally and rightly criticized. I refer to the gross overcrowding in prisons. Three factors have been predominant here.

(1) A remorseless increase in crime.
(2) The heavy sentences passed by the judiciary, very severe by European standards.
(3) The lack of resources, human and material, for which the government of the day must bear the primary responsibility.

If we had a more forgiving society, the judges would not feel that they had to reflect such harsh public attitudes. The government would be brave enough, one hopes, to increase the numbers of prison officers and in particular of probation officers. The latter would be indispensable in any extension of alternatives to prison. It would need a more forgiving attitude to make these non-custodian alternatives acceptable. But even if overcrowding were miraculously abolished overnight, deeper underlying problems would remain. I will illustrate them from three long-term prisoners very well known to me.

The first was convicted over twenty years ago of horrific crimes against children. Not long afterwards a top government psychiatrist concluded that he was a mental case and should be sent to Broadmoor, the top security hospital. The Home Secretary was willing but the Minister of Health prevented it at the time. Fourteen years later, he was eventually transferred to a top security hospital in the north of England. He is a gifted man, who started life with everything against him and somehow managed to acquire an impressive knowledge of writers like Tolstoy, Dostoevsky, and William Blake. But an unforgiving society and a blinkered Minister prevented the proper attention being given to this extaordinary individual.

How does forgiveness relate itself to the mental offender? I pose the question rather than attempting to answer it, except to suggest that there are enlightened doctors who have not yet been given their chance to cope with the problem.

Another prisoner, the young accomplice of the one just described has, like him, been imprisoned for over twenty years. No-one supposes that she is in any way dangerous. The local review committee, including the governor of her prison, considered some while ago that she ought to be released on licence (equivalent to parole). She is deeply religious and full of remorse. But public opinion, whipped up by the tabloid press at its worst, is understood to be so hostile to her that no Home Secretary would dare to release her. For many years she hid from herself and the authorities the full truth about the crimes in which she was involved. She has since proved her repentance by her total commitment to the search for the bodies of two further victims, one of which has been found. Also she has twice been taken with her full consent to the moors, the scene of the crimes. She has asked to be hypnotized. And she has won the confidence of a succession of Catholic priests and a Methodist minister (a former prison governor) who has helped her much. Whatever the attitude of the public and whatever her treatment by the authorities, she will have to live with the recollection of her crime. She is secure in the conviction that God has forgiven her, but faces the prospect of a lifelong atonement.

Third, I will take a young man from Derry in Northern Ireland. He came of a most respectable family. His father was the headmaster of a leading grammar school; his seven brothers and sisters had all gone to college. He was doing extremely well at school. Then came Bloody Sunday when British paratroopers shot and killed fourteen demonstrators. He joined the IRA; he was soon distributing letter bombs. At least a dozen of the recipients were damaged, two of them losing a hand; eventually he was caught and sentenced to life imprisonment. After fourteen years he is still in prison. What makes his story remarkable (unique in my experience) is not only his remorse and repudiation of all violence, but his insistance on apologies being sent to his victims. This is not such an easy matter as it sounds. The Home Office officials looked in vain for a precedent. Eventually the Catholic priests at Wormwood Scrubs procured permission to approach whatever victims could be discovered. Some accepted the apologies gratefully, others declined, but the purpose of the prisoner could only be described (in the words of Robert Louis Stevenson) as that of the 'true penitent'. His attitude required a good deal of courage, moral, and physical. He had to live with IRA colleagues who might have made his life a hell. As far as I know, they did not do so. He stuck it out, and at the time of writing, has been offered a place at Cambridge University.

But has all this done him any good with the authorities? There are no signs that it has. It may be said that he had no right to expect any response and up to a point that is a reasonable comment. But the whole parole system is theoretically based on the idea that when a prisoner provides evidence of moral regeneration, his chance of release is improved.

I conclude without hesitation that the lack of forgiveness in high places or a fear in high places of a lack of public forgiveness, have been responsible for this young man's continuing detention. Therefore, I am submitting that if, as a society, we had a more forgiving attitude our prison system would look much more Christian than it does today.

Conclusions

This book is much shorter than the one I originally intended, or even the one which I had in mind when I wrote the Introduction. I have long had the feeling that there was a gap in the best discussions of forgiveness, but, had not expected to find it such a yawning gulf. I started with the idea that forgiveness, like humility, was a distinctive Christian quality, that it was inseparable from the life and teaching of Jesus Christ. I have been surprised not to find closer analogies in the philosophies and the other great religions. That is true even of Judaism to which Christianity owes a debt which can never be emphasized too strongly.

In an Interlude (see pages 27-28) I have indicated the limitations of Islam in the same connection. As far as I can make out the other religions have still less to offer. Nearly all the best thinkers, theological and philosophical, have, at some point or other, recommended the rejection of long-standing resentment *in the interests of the victim*. The philosopher Seneca was once asked why he did not retaliate when someone insulted him. He is said to have replied: 'If a donkey kicked you, would you kick it back?' This is a long way from the Christian instruction to love one's enemies and to pray for those who persecute one. I had expected, moreover, to devote one or two chapters to the developement of Christian thought about forgiveness since the dissemination of the Gospel. I had hoped to find much of interest in Augustine, Aquinas and in Luther, for instance, not to mention modern theologians: but I have been sadly disappointed in that, at least as far as *forgiveness of man by man* is concerned.

Forgiveness of man by God has, admittedly, been argued about over the centuries, sometimes with unhappy results. Even in that area I have found myself being referred back repeatedly to Professor Mackintosh's *Christian Experience of Forgiveness* first published in 1927. The *Christian Dictionary of Ethics* published in 1983 includes a masterly review of the subject by Paul Lehmann, but it does not carry us much further than the earlier thesis.

Paul Lehmann like other writers deals very briefly with forgiveness of man by man (as did Mackintosh). He still leaves unsolved such problems as those I shall turn to in a moment. He admits somewhat ruefully that the discussion of forgiveness in the literature of Christian theology and ethics is conspicuously slight.

In short, the instinctive reaction to a shattering outrage of heart-and-soul Christians like Gordon Wilson and Mr Gormley is much the same today as it would have been in the first century AD. It is not dissimilar to that of Stephen at the beginning of the Christian story who called out while being stoned to death, 'Lay not this sin to their charge.'

I have, in a small way, carried out some inductive research into forgiveness, recorded above. I have explored what forgiveness and its opposite have meant in a number of cases. The answers have been, as might be expected, immensely varied but surely it would be the same if we were exploring courage or loyalty. My samples are obviously too small to permit confident generalizations. Much work remains to be done by Christians and psychologists working together and, indeed, by collaboration between all caring persons.

In the text I have quoted the psychological view that forgiveness must not be too hastily imposed on the afflicted. No doubt there is an element of truth in this. I retain, however, the conviction that anyone who is himself a Christian and is trying to help a victim will hope and pray that the victim will come in time to forgive.

If the theologians have not given us positive guidance in regard to the practical application of forgiveness it is left to each of us to make our own endeavours. I will take just three of the problems confronting us, all of which I touched on in the Introduction.

First: Is it possible to forgive anyone who has not harmed us directly or indirectly?

The Vicar of Ealing, as we have seen, immediately forgave those who had beaten him up but would not have thought it right for him to try to forgive those who had raped the young woman. I am ready to believe that he forgave those concerned the distress occasioned *him* by her maltreatment but left it to her, with God's help, to forgive those who had so cruelly abused her.

I cannot withhold my sympathy for his attitude and yet it does not seem to me the whole truth. I am driven to conclude that forgiveness in its original form refers to forgiving those who have injured us but that the teaching of Christ leads ineluctably to extend the idea much more widely.

The question becomes acute when we turn to community forgiveness, for instance in the case of Northern Ireland or the Jewish response to the Holocaust. Those who inflicted the atrocities are in many cases dead (always dead in the case of historic wrongs). Those who represent the 'victim community' have in many cases not suffered themselves. Here again I think that we must extend the original idea of forgiveness, just as we extend the idea of justice between man and man to social justice in the community. It seems to me inconceivable that a Christian on reflection will rule out the idea of community forgiveness.

The second problem is the question of whether it is a duty to forgive someone before he or she has repented.

It would certainly be possible by a manipulation of New Testament texts to arrive at a negative answer. But when Jesus Christ said to Peter that each of us must forgive his neighbour up to seventy times seven I would take that to mean indefinitely, which in turn rules out the notion of waiting until the neighbour has repented. When Christ said on the cross, ' Father, forgive them', it was an unqualified request, not one dependent on the attitude of those who needed to be forgiven. It is true that he added, 'for they know not what they do', but this points the way in my eyes to the general reflection that none of us can be sure of the knowledge and motives of present-day offenders. A further consideration weighs with me a good deal. In half a century of prison visiting I have been asked repeatedly whether such-and-such a prisoner feels remorse or has repented. Sometimes I can give a confident affirmative answer, but speaking broadly none of us are capable of judging the degree of repentance or remorse of our fellow human beings.

Thirdly, and most difficult, is the whole problem of combining forgiveness with punishment. I have dealt with this issue in Chapter 8. My answer, simplified, amounts to this. Punishment is part of Christian justice, but sentences and the administration of justice in prison, for example, must at all times be guided by love. An impossible aspiration, if you like, but the only standard by which to judge a penal system.

To hate the sin and to love the sinner has been for me at all times essential wisdom.

A devil's advocate may here ask whether I am placing forgiveness on the same footing as other impossible injunctions in the Sermon on the Mount such as the command to 'resist not evil' and to turn the other cheek. Not so, although I admit that the distinction is hard to draw between one Divine instruction and another. I would suggest myself that the instructions not to resist evil and to turn the other cheek must be applied in conjunction with other aspects of Christian teaching. The instruction to forgive is absolute and binding in all circumstances.

I turn finally to the question of whether forgiveness is anything other than a repetition of Christ's commandment to love our neighbour as we love ourselves. In a sense that is true, but forgiveness relates that fundamental instruction to circumstances in which it is particularly hard to carry it out. It is not *natural* to forgive those who injure us, still less natural to forgive those who injure or even kill those we love. Christ tells us, and places the authority of His life and death behind the instruction, that here our natural instinct must be transcended by something higher, something more spiritual. Everybody, Christian and non-Christian, has surely an inkling that this possibility lies within all of us. Everyone, Christian or non-Christian, is capable of responding to the Christian message of forgiveness whether delivered by Her Majesty the Queen in a Christmas broadcast, or in the witness of the humblest victim.

The true apostles of forgiveness are those who exemplify in their lives. Gordon Wilson of Enniskillen and countless others have proved that here and elsewhere deeds are far more eloquent than words. I myself have never suffered the wrongs which would have given me the opportunity to present myself as a forgiving man and can have no idea how I would have responded to the challenge. At least I have pursued in public and private, especially in dealing with Germany and prisoners, a policy of forgiving those whom the world finds it hardest to forgive. Real Christianity would no doubt have called for much more persistence and courage on my part. It would certainly not have demanded less.

Postscript

As prisoners, we came to find that we were amazed by the liberating power of an increasing realization that our captors were truly men who did not know what they were doing. We developed a kind of pity for our dangerously erratic guards because they and their masters seemed to us to be the prisoners in some deep, ancient oubliette of the human spirit, and we the free in hearts and minds.

From 'Tolerance through Torment'
by Laurens van der Post in
The Times, 25 January 1989

EPILOGUE

Forgiveness and public policy

The foregoing text was published in 1989. In the meanwhile the world has moved on as fast as ever. The Christian message about forgiveness does not change, however, nor has the interpretation been obviously modified. There was no book in the English language on forgiveness of man by man when I published mine in 1989. Nor, as far as I am aware, has one appeared since. In a general way, therefore, I do not feel the need to alter what I wrote at that time.

A good deal more could have been said about the damaging effects on a human being of not forgiving. In that connection President Nixon whom I came to know and respect after his downfall provides a good example of the opposite. President Nixon at the moment of his disgrace made the resolve not to entertain feelings of bitterness and resentment against those who had destroyed his Presidency. He faithfully kept his promise. As was generally recognised when he died.

But there is a wider issue which has become much clearer to me since then. Private forgiveness is one thing and public forgiveness is another, although they are inextricably intertwined.

No event on the forgiveness front has been more striking since I wrote than the noble forgiveness extended by the widow of the murdered headmaster to her husband's murderer. Our political leaders were quick to show a new zeal for a moral regeneration. But in public discussion there has been no reference to forgiveness as a factor, for example, in dealing with criminals.

In my lifetime there have been three occasions when forgiveness played or should have played a considerable part in determining policy.

When I went out to Germany in the summer of 1947 as Minister for the British zone, a powerful lead in the direction of forgiveness had already been given by noble figures like Bishop Bell, Bishop of Chichester, Victor Gollancz who then called himself a Judeo/Christian and Dick Stokes, Catholic M.P. decorated for valour in the earlier war.

I delivered that message to the best of my ability. I told the half-starving children of Dusseldorf, 'You're absolutely right to be proud of being Germans. Never believe that the whole world is against you' (which in retrospect sounds like economy of the truth). When I returned to London I was asked whether I minded having a public relations officer with me on my next visit. Mine was far from the official line. I tried to resign, sending a heartfelt letter to my much-admired Prime Minister Clem Attlee. He replied 'My dear Frank, I have received your note and will try to look into it later if I have time.' I lapsed into impotence. Like the disciples at Gethsemane the spirit was willing. The flesh was weak. In the end the Cold War assuaged the conscience of the West.

The long-term effect of private forgiveness on public forgiveness is incalculable. The same can be said of the historic act of forgiveness performed by the draper of Enniskillen when he forgave the murderers of his daughter. The same can surely be said of the long-term effects of the forgiveness extended by Erskine Childers in 1922 to those who ordered and those who carried out his execution.

Erskine Childers, whom I have described elsewhere as the last great Anglo-Irishman, took the Republican side in the Civil War. He was arrested in possession of a small revolver given him by Michael Collins and in due course shot at dawn, He insisted on shaking hands with his executioners. And not only that, he made his son, then at Haileybury College, promise to shake hands with those who ordered the execution. This in due course his son did and eventually became a President of the Irish Republic.

In this Epilogue I would hope to stimulate the beginnings of a serious discussion about the relationship of private to public forgiveness. The Christian message of forgiveness preached for the first time by Christ is plain enough. 'Forgive us our trespasses as we forgive those who trespass against us.' We should forgive up to seventy times seven, in other words indefinitely. 'Father forgive them for they know not what they do.' The first two exhortations are directed to each one of us as individuals, the third to us collectively. In the last few years forgiveness has not had all its own way.

This is not the place to dwell, however briefly, on the story of the War Crimes Bill. For understandable reasons the initiative was Jewish. It came from a dedicated Jewish organization which had pursued for many years the aim of prosecuting war criminals. It became accepted Conservative party policy. It was rejected twice by the House of Lords where the overwhelming opinion prevailed that no fair trial was possible after all these years. The whole of the legal establishment was against it and for my part I denounced it in the name of forgiveness. In the end the House of Commons prevailed but at the time of writing it has been possible to discover only one 85-year-old alleged war criminal to prosecute. It is about as discredited as any piece of modern legislation.

In a minor way I have tried to do my best for victims, opening the first debate about them in the House of Lords and introducing the first Private Member's Bill on their behalf. I am President of the Matthew Trust which is much concerned with victims. But such efforts fade into insignificance when set against the indescribable sufferings of the Jews and other victims in recent years.

I am aware that loyalty to the dead, itself a noble emotion, will always make it almost impossible for many Jews to forgive the perpetrators of the Holocaust. In the face of such feelings one can only bow one's head in respectful silence. But injustice must be pursued objectively if painfully.

In the foregoing text I have examined at some length, after first-hand enquiries, the attitude of Jewish theologians to forgiveness of man by man. Like Christian theologians they do not speak with one voice. On moral questions there is no one listened to in the House of Lords more carefully than the former Chief Rabbi Dr Jacobowitz. In the debate initiated by the Archbishop of Canterbury in July 1996 on the need for a moral renewal, Dr Jacobowitz was much admired. But on 14 December 1995 he published an article in the *Daily Mail* entitled WHY WE SHOULD DAMN THIS DISASTROUS URGE TO FORGIVE. The fact that it was strongly supported in a leading article does not make it any less lamentable in my eyes. But as I have shown earlier, another eminent Rabbi demonstrated an attitude to forgiveness similar to that of Christians, though he claims that it derived from the Talmud rather than the Gospels.

It is impossible to discuss forgiveness in 1997 as compared with 1989 without referring to the traumatic change in British penal policy which will always be associated with the coming of Michael Howard to the Home Office in 1993.

There had been six Home Secretaries preceding him who varied in their attachment to penal progress but in the event the Act of 1991 continued the general movement towards a more humane system which I had witnessed since I first visited prisons in the late 1930s.

At the Conservative Conference in October 1993 Michael Howard, strongly supported by the Prime Minister, announced a totally new approach. Offenders were to be treated worse and victims better. The first part of that plan has been vigorously pursued but the Government's initial proposals for treating victims were hailed with contempt and condemned as unlawful by the judiciary. Howardism, as I have come to call it, consists of two main tenets: prison works and it will work still better if made more unpleasant for prisoners. The number in prison has already increased substantially under Howardism. This is at time when the numbers of the prison service and the probation service are being severely cut.

Plans to increase the number of prisoners sharply are embodied in the Crime Sentences Act which at the time of writing, 8 May 1997, has recently passed into law. It is possible to hope that it will never be operated by a Labour Government. The Labour leadership in the Commons were very mild in their criticisms of it on the eve of the General Election. But they were hostile to it in the Lords as were the Liberal Democrats, the former Conservative Home Office ministers and the judiciary.

The Prison Governors Association have issued a dramatic denunciation of the new doctrine. The Prison Service as a whole and the Probation Service had been equally critical.

The last Chief Inspector was a declared opponent of Howardism. If Mr Howard expected his successor, a distinguished soldier, to be more amenable, he picked the wrong man.

The Crime Sentences Act was strongly critized in the Commons by two former Conservative Home Secretaries – Mr Douglas Hurd and Mr Kenneth Baker and also by a former Minister of State at the Home Office, Sir Peter Lloyd, now the admired Chairman of the New Bridge for ex-prisoners. Mr Douglas Hurd has since become Chairman of the Prison Reform Trust, whose penal ideals are in flagrant contradiction to those of Mr Howard, and entered the House of Lords. Forgiveness has not been the word much used by the critics but a measure of it, at least, is involved in their determined stand for the rehabilitation ideal.

But what of the voting public whom the exponents of Howardism assume to be demanding a harsher attitude to criminals? How can they be persuaded that the idea of forgiving criminals should play a serious part in their ethical approach?

Nothing on the face of it has been more opposed to the whole spirit of forgiveness than public policy towards Myra Hindley. Already imprisoned for more than thirty years, she was informed by the recent Home Secretary that she is one of a small number of prisoners who must expect to die in prison. She was convicted for her share in the appalling Moors murders when she was in fact the infatuated accomplice of Ian Brady, whom she worked under in the office. Before she met him she was a good Catholic girl of eighteen.

Brought up in poor circumstances without knowing who his father was and going to borstals in adolescence, the strangely gifted but mentally afflicted Ian Brady acquired an excellent knowledge of Russian literature for example. When I published some of his letters a leading professor wrote to me 'He must be a remarkable man.' He has now for many years been in a special hospital.

By the time I first met Myra Hindley in prison, two years after the crimes, she had already returned to her religion. Priest after priest has testified to the fact that she has become a good religious woman, as has the Reverend Peter Timms, former governor of Maidstone Prison and now a Methodist minister. But the tabloid press has over the years presented her as a hate figure to the public. It is widely said that no Home Secretary would dare to let her out. Yet the Parole Board has recently recommended she should go to an open prison, which is generally regarded as a step towards freedom.

So there we have it: all knowledge on one side of the argument and tabloid vilification and political timidity on the other.

Today the letters that reach me are far more favourable than unfavourable. One must hope and pray that slowly but surely forgiveness will do its work.

So what is my last word about forgiveness in public policy? For Christians and those who accept Christian ethics, forgiveness must emerge as an interpretation of the direct guidance Christ gave to individuals from his last words to those concerned with his crucifixion. The great difficulty in my prolonged experience which holds back decent people from allowing forgiveness to enter into punishment is the feeling deep down that it conflicts with condemnation, that it leads us to be soft on crime. Saint Augustine once and for all pointed us in the right direction. We must condemn the sin but love the sinner. Yet what meaning can be attached to the injunction to love those we have never seen in the flesh though we may have read about their horrible deeds? My noble-minded friend Victor Gollancz, mentioned in the text, when we were discussing the need to love our enemies, announced, 'I adore Hitler' which was felt to be going too far. But at least we can put aside bitterness and hatred and in that sense allow forgiveness to play its part in public policy. A taxi driver not long ago told me that he felt cheated of his revenge when he heard that Fred West had committed suicide but he rejected such feelings because he knew that they were strong. Society will take a step forward when collectively we follow the example of the taxi driver and begin to move closer to Christ.

The above was written before the result was known of the British Election of 1997. Most of the Prime Ministers of recent years have been Christians but not since Gladstone in the nineteenth century has there been a Prime Minister so explicitly committed to Christianity as Tony Blair. So my last words in the book on Forgiveness are those of hope.